NUMBER 393

THE ENGLISH
EXPERIENCE

ITS RECORD IN EARLY PRINTED BOOKS
PUBLISHED IN FACSIMILE

EDWARD JORDEN

A DISCOVRSE OF
NATVRALL BATHES
AND MINERALL WATERS

LONDON 1631

DA CAPO PRESS
THEATRVM ORBIS TERRARVM LTD.
AMSTERDAM 1971 NEW YORK

The publishers acknowledge their gratitude
to the Curators of the Bodleian Library, Oxford
for their permission to reproduce
the Library's copy (Shelfmark: Gough Somers 39)
and to the Trustees of the British Museum
for their permission to reproduce
the pages from the Library's copy
(Shelfmark: 234.h.29)
Library of Congress Catalog Card Number:
70-171769

S.T.C. No. 14791
Collation: A-M^4, N^2

Published in 1971 by
Theatrum Orbis Terrarum Ltd.,
O.Z. Voorburgwal 85, Amsterdam

&

Da Capo Press
- a division of Plenum Publishing Corporation -
227 West 17th Street, New York, 10011
Printed in the Netherlands
ISBN 90 221 0393 5

DISCOVRSE

OF

NATVRALL BATHES,
AND
MINERALL WATERS.

Wherein firſt the originall of Fountaines in generall is declared.

Then the nature and differences of Minerals, with examples of particular Bathes from moſt of them.

Next the generation of Minerals in the earth, from whence both the actuall heate of Bathes, and their vertues are proued to proceede.

Alſo by what meanes Minerall Waters are to be examined and diſcouered.

And laſtly, of the nature and vſes of Bathes, but eſpecially of our Bathes at *Bathe* in *Sommerſetſhire*.

By ED. IORDEN *Dr. in Phyſicke.*

LONDON:
Printed by THOMAS HARPER,
1631.

TO THE RIGHT
HONOVRABLE, SIR
F<small>RANCIS</small> C<small>OTTINGTON</small>, Bar-
ronet, Chancellour of the Exchequer, and
one of his Maiesties moſt Honourable
Priuy C<small>OVNCELL</small>.

He profitable vſe of Bathes, both for neceſſity and comfort, is ſuch, and ſo well confirmed from all antiquity, as I need not labour to illuſtrate it more; onely it hath beene the ill hap of our Country Bathes to lye more obſcure then any other throughout Chriſtendome, although they deſerue as well as the beſt, becauſe very few haue written any thing of them, and thoſe haue either not mentioned, or but ſlightly paſſed ouer the maine points concerning their cauſes and originals; contenting themſelues with an empericall vſe of them. This hath made me through the inſtigation alſo of ſome of my worthy friends, to attempt ſomewhat in this kinde : which if it giue not ſatisfaction according to my deſire, yet it may be a prouocation to ſome others, to perfect that which I haue begun. And ſeeing I doe it for the vſe of my Country, I haue neglected curious ornaments to garniſh it withall, but haue clad it in a plaine ſuit of our country Cloath, without welt or gard : not deſiring it ſhould ſhew it ſelfe in forraine parts: *Mea cymba legat littus.*

But in this mine vndertaking, I finde my ſelfe expoſed to many cenſures, both concerning ſome paradoxicall opinions in Philoſophy, which notwithſtanding I deliuer not *gratis*, but confirmed with good grounds of reaſon and authorities: as alſo concerning the reformation of our Bathes, which doe daily ſuffer many indignities more waies then I haue mentioned, vnder the tyranny of ignorance, impoſture, priuate reſpects, wants, factions, diſorder, &c. ſo as they are not able to diſplay their vertues, and doe that good for which God hath ſent them to vs: and all for want of ſuch good gouernement as other Bathes doe enioy. I blame not our City herein, vnto whoſe care the ordering of theſe Bathes is committed, the diſorders and defects being ſuch as are out of their verge, and neither in their power, nor in their knowledge to redreſſe. For they haue ſufficiently teſtified their

deſire of reforming all ſuch abuſes, when they
voluntarily did ioyne in petitioning the late
King *Iames* of bleſſed memory, to that end :
by whoſe death this petition alſo dyed. And
they knew well that it muſt be ſuperiour power
that muſt effeſt it. In theſe reſpeſts I haue need
of ſome noble and eminent Patron to proteſt
both me and my Bathes, whoſe cauſe I take
vpon me to plead, and to aduance, according
to their due deſert: but eſpecially for the Bathes
ſake, which I deſire may flouriſh to the vtmoſt
extent of benefit to the people; and to haue all
impediments remoued out of their way, which
may hinder them in the progreſſe of their vertues. This is the cauſe Sir, why I preſume to
dedicate theſe my labours to your Honour,
who hauing obſerued in forraigne parts, the
vſes and gouernements of all ſorts, and being
both by the fauour of his Maieſtie well able,
and by your noble diſpoſition well inclined
and willing to maintaine good order and diſ-
cipline, will, I doubt not, excuſe this boldneſſe, and pardon my preſumption. Conſider
Sir, that this is your natiue Country, which
naturally euery man doth affeſt to aduance;
and theſe Bathes are the principall Iewels of
your Country, & able to make it more famous

then any other parts of this Kingdome, and in aduancing them, to aduance your name to all poſterity. Wherefore howſoeuer my ſelfe deſerue but ſmall reſpect from you, yet I beſeech you reſpect the Bathes of your Country, and me as a welwiſher vnto them.

And as the common opinion of your great worth and abilities, haue moued mee to this boldneſſe, ſo the particular fauours of your Noble Lady, and the encouragement of your learned Phyſitian, Maſter Docter *Baſkeruill,* mine eſpeciall friend, who hath ſpurred mee on to this worke, haue remoued out of my minde all ſuſpition of miſconſtruction. But that as mine intent hath beene meerely the enlarging of the knowledge of thoſe poynts concerning Bathes, and more eſpecially of our Bathes in Sommerſetſhire; ſo you will be pleaſed to accept of this publike inuitation by mee to doe your Country good, and your ſelfe honour, which I wiſh may neuer be diſioyned. And to mee it will be no ſmall encouragement to deuote my ſelfe and my beſt endeauours to your ſeruice. So I humbly take leaue this **23**. *Aprilis* 1 6 3 1.

Your Lordſhips moſt humble Seruant,

Lbellum istum DE AQVIS MEDICA-
TIS, à Doctissimo IORDANO antiquissi-
mo Collega nostro scriptum multiplici erudi-
tione & nouarum subtilitatum varia supellectile re-
fertissimum, legimus, & qui ab omnibus tam Phi-
losophis quam Medicis legatur dignissimum iudi-
cauimus.

IOHANNES ARGENT Collegij Medicorum
Londinensium Præsidens.

IOHANNES GIFFORD.
SIMON BASKERVILLE.
THOMAS RIDGELEY.

In laudem operis.

Parue alacri passu liber, Liber, ibis in orbem;
  Dentesque spernes liuidos.
Authores pandit, sua dat Iordenus, & vsu
  Quæsita multo protulit.
Aëra qui totus, Flammas meditatur, & vndas,
  Terram, metalla discutit.
Quicquid in his veteres, docuit quicquid Nouus Author,
  Celeri notauit pollice.
At sua dum exponit, lucem dat, operta recludit,
  Pennáque fertur libera.
Perge liber: gratus gratum volueris in Æuum
  Lymphæ calentes dum fluent.

Ed. Lapworth, M. D.

In laudem Authoris.

Numine diuino Iordan medicabile flumen
  Dicitur, è gelido licèt illud frigore constet :
Tu Iordane decus medicorum, candide Doctor,
Lumine diuino gnarus discernere causas
Ægris corporibus nôsti depellere morbos;
Intima seclusæ penetrâsti viscera terræ,
Thermarum vires aperis, reserasque metalla :
De gremio Telluris aquas manare fluentes
Qua ratione doces, nobis priùs abdita pandis
Scrutando Physices arcana indogine mira,
Nec caperis famâ, nec inani laudis amore,
Vt patriæ prosis, dignarus promere lucem :
Qui memorauerunt, vel qui modò Balnea tractant,
Non sunt te meliùs meriti, vel iudice Momo.

Io. Dauntesey.

OF
NATVRALL
BATHES,
AND
MINERALL WATERS.

Cap. i.

Explication of the word Bathe. The scope and argument
of this Booke. The ancient vse and esteeme of Bathes a-
mong the Romans. The moderne vse of them among the
Turkes. Of medicinable Bathes, and minerall Waters. How
esteemed by Greekes, Latines, Arabians, & other nations.

HE word *Bathe* or *Balneum* is of
larger extent then I purpose to dif-
course of : for it being the name of
a forme of remedie applied to the
body, it may be framed either out of
liquid things, or solid substances, or
vapours.

Liquid Substances are Water, Milke, Must, Wine,

B   Oyles

Oyle: folid fubftances are Sand, Salt, preffed Grapes, Corne, &c. vapours are Stuffes and hot houfes.

My intent is onely to treate of waters, and principally of thofe which be called Minerall, whether they bee vfed in Bath or in Potion, &c.

Pancirollus de deperditis. Thefe kinde of watrie Bathes haue beene in vfe from all antiquity, and held in great efteeme. Among the ancient Romans there were no Buildings more magnificent then their Bathes, whereof there are reported to haue beene in *Rome,* 856. The chiefeft of thefe were the *Anthonin,* and *Dioclefian* Bathes; the walles whereof were of admirable height, with an infinite number of marble Pillars, erected for oftentation, and not to fupport any thing, 1000 Seates to fit in; Their *Caldaria, Lepidaria, Frigidaria,* moft fumptuous and ftately : the whole fabricke fo large and fpacious, as they refembled rather Cities then Houfes. And fo it might well be, when as there were imployed for the building of the *Dioclefian* Bathes, as *Baccius* faith, 4000. men, but *Salmuth* faith, 14000. for fome yeares together. They were placed where now the Church of Saint *Angelo* ftands.

Rollorius obfervat: liv, 3. cap: 34. The Turkes at this day retaine that ancient cuftome of the Romans, and are in nothing more profufe, then in their Temples and Bathes, which are like vnto great Pallaces, and in euery Citie very frequent: And yet both the Romans and the Turkes vfed thofe Bathes onely for pleafure, and delicacy, and cleanlineffe : the Romans going barelegged, and their waies dufty, had need of often wafhing: and the Turkes lying in their cloathes, fubiect to Lice and wormes, if it were not for their often bathing.

Now if thofe Nations would beftow fo much vpon their Bathes of delicacie and pleafure, which were onely of pure water; wee haue much more reafon to adorne

out

our minerall Bathes; which (befides the former vfes)are alfo medicinall and very foueraigne for many difeafes, confifting of wholefome minerals, and approued for many hundred yeares, of many who could not otherwife be recouered. At the leaft wife if wee doe not beautifie and adorne them, yet we fhould fo accommodate them, as they might ferue for the vtmoft extent of benefit to fuch as neede them.

For there is nothing in our profeffion of Phyficke more vfefull, nor in the workes of nature more admirable, (man onely excepted, which *Plato* cals the great miracle) then naturall Bathes, and minerall Waters. The nature and caufes whereof haue beene fo hard to difcouer, as our ancient Authors haue written little of them, holding them to be facred or holy, either for that they iudged them to haue their vertue immediately from God, or at leaft from the celeftiall Bodies; from whence, both their actuall heate was thought to be kindled, by lightnings or fuch like impreffions, and other admirable vertues, and fometimes contrary effects deriued, which appeare in them: Alfo diuers miracles haue beene afcribed vnto thofe naturall Bathes, to confirme the opinion of a fupernaturall power in them, as *Guaynerius* reports of the Bathes of *Aque* in *Italy:* and *Langius* out of *Athenæus,* concerning the Bathes of *Edepfus,* which both loft their vertue for a time. The one by the Magiftrates prohibiting poore difeafed people to vfe them, the other by impofing a taxation vpon them. but vpon the reformation of thofe abufes, were reftored to their former vertues againe.

Cap 2.
Epift. 53. lib. 2.

I neede not herein auerring the opinion of Diuinitie which was held to be in Bathes, make any mention of the Poole of *Bethefda,* written of by Saint *Iohn,* and *Nonnus* the Poet:nor of the riuer *Iordan,* which cured

Naman the *Aſſyrian* of his Leproſie: being indeede true
miracles, and done by a ſupernaturall power : yet it is
likely that thoſe and ſuch like examples bred in the
mindes of men a reuerend and diuine opinion of all
Bathes: eſpecially where they ſaw ſuch ſtrange effects as
they could not well reduce to naturall cauſes.

And this hath beene the cauſe that in old time theſe
minerall fountaines haue beene conſecrated vnto certaine dieties: as *Hamon* in *Libya*, vnto *Iupiter* : *Thermo-
pyla*, vnto *Hercules*, by *Lallas* among the *Troglodits*,
another to the *Sun*, &c. And at this day we haue diuers
Bathes which carry the names of Sunne, Moone, and
Saints: and many Townes and Cities named from the
Bathes in them: as *Therma* in *Macedonia* & *Sicily*, *Ther-
midea* in *Rhodes*, *Aqua* in *Italy*, *Aquiſgran* in *Germany*, *Baden* in *Heluetia*: and our ancient Citie of Bathe in
Sommerſetſhire, in honour whereof I haue eſpecially
vndertaken this labour, and I perſwade my ſelfe, that a-
mong the infinite number of Bathes and minerall waters which are in Europe, there are none of more vniuer-
ſall vſe for curing of diſeaſes, nor any more commodious
for entertainement of ſicke perſons, then theſe are.

Beſides this ſacred conceit of Bathes, wherewith in
ancient times, the mindes of men were poſſeſt, we may
adde this, that the nature of Minerals was not ſo well
diſcouered by them, as it hath beene ſince : and therefore wee finde very little written of this argument, either in *Ariſtotle* or *Ippocrates*, or in *Galen*, who wrote
moſt copiouſly in all other points of Phyſicke, yet concerning this hath little; and neuer gaue any of theſe waters to drinke inwardly, although hee acknowledgeth
that they were in vſe: and for outward vſes, held them
all to be potentially hot.

After theſe Grecians, the ancient Latines and Ara-

*De tuenda ſa-
nit. lib.4.cap.4.*

bians fucceeded : *Pliny, Celfus, Seneca, Lucretius, Aui-cen, Rhafis, Seraphio, Auerrhoes,* in whom wee finde fome fmall mention of naturall Bathes, and fome vfe of Salt and nitrous, and Aluminous waters, but nothing of worth towards the difcouerie of the naturall caufes of them. It is likely they did paffe it ouer flightly, either by reafon of the difficulty in fearching out the caufes of them, or that they iudged them meerely metaphyficall. But in later times the nature and generation of Minerals (from whom the Bathes proceede, and from whence the Bathes proceede, and from whence the whole doctrine of them both for their qualities, and differences, origi-nals and vfe, muft be deriued) being better looked into, and obferuations taken from fuch as daily labour in the bowels of the earth, for the fearch of Mines, or fuch as afterwards prepare them for our neceffarie vfes; we haue attayned to better knowledge in this kinde, then the Ancients could haue, although in all new difcoueries there will be defects for fucceeding ages to fupply, fo it fals out in this: *Dies Diem docet: Alpham Beta corrigit.* And although *Agricola, Fullopius, Baccius, Mathefius, Solinander, Libanius,* &c. haue added much vnto that which was formerly knowne in this point, and refor-med many errors and miftakings in former writers: yet they haue left many things imperfect, doubtfull, ob-fcure, controuerted, and perhaps falfe, as may appeare in the difcourfe following. I doe reuerence all their worths, as from whom I haue learned many things which elfe I could hardly haue attained vnto; and I ac-knowledge them to haue beene excellent inftruments for the aduancement of learning : yet I hope it may bee as free for me without imputation of arrogancie to pub-lifh my conceits herein, as it hath beene for them, or may be for any other: *Hanc veniam petimufque damuf-*

que viciſſim. My end and ſtudie is the common good, and the bettering of this knowledge: and if I ſhall bring any further light to increaſe that, I ſhall be glad : otherwiſe my intent being to ſearch out the truth, and not to contradict others, it will or ought to be a ſufficient protection for mee, wherefore I come to diſcourſe of Minerall waters.

CAP. 2.

Definition of Minerall waters. The nature whereof cannot be vnderſtood, except firſt conſideration be had concerning ſimple water. Of which in this Chapter are ſhewed the qualities and vſe.

Libauius de iudicio aquarum miner. cap. 1.

Minerall waters are ſuch, as beſides their owne ſimple nature, haue receiued and imbibed ſome other qualitie or ſubſtance from Subterraneall Mynes. I ſay, beſides their owne nature, becauſe they retaine ſtill their liquidneſſe and cold, and moyſture, although for a time they may be actually hot from an externall impreſſion of heate, which being gone, they returne to their former cold againe. I ſay imbybed, to diſtinguiſh them from confuſed waters : as earth may bee confuſed with water, but not imbybed, and will ſinke to the bottome againe: whereas ſuch things as are imbybed, are ſo mixed with the water, as it retaines them, and is vnited with it: being either Spirits, or diſſoluble Iuyces, or tinctures; I ſay from Subterraneall mynes, to diſtinguiſh them from animall or vegetable ſubſtances, as infuſions or decoctions of hearbs, fleſh, &c.

Seeing then that the Baſis of theſe Bathes or minerall fountaines, is water, we muſt firſt conſider the nature of ſimple water, and from thence wee ſhall better iudge of

Minerall Waters and their differences.

By fimple water I doe not meane the Element of wa- *Baccius lib.1.*
ter, for that is no where to be found among mixt bodies, *cap.6.*
but I meane fuch water as is free from any heterogeneall *Solinander lib.1 cap. 1.*
admixture, which may alter either the touch or tafte, or
colour, or fmell, or weight, or confiftence, or any other
qualitie, which may be difcerned either by the fenfes, or
by the effects. This water therefore muft haue his proper colour and tafte, without fauour, or fmell, thin, light,
cold, and moyft; if any of thefe properties be wanting,
or any redownd, it is mixed and infected.

Cold and moyfture doe abound in water more then *Solinander lib 1.*
in any other Element. For cold appeares by this, that *cap.3.*
being heated by any externall caufe, it foone returnes to
his cold nature againe, when the caufe of the heate is remoued. And whereas Ayre is held by the Stoicks to be *Queft.nat.2.*
moft cold, and confirmed by *Seneca*, and *Libanius*, yet *Libau.pyrotech. cap.20.*
the reafon they giue for it, doth proue water to bee
more cold, becaufe they make the matter of ayre to bee
water, and to haue his coldnefle from thence. But *Ari-* *Meteor.4.*
ftotle holds the ayre to be hot from the efficient caufe
which rarefied it, being of more validitie to make it hot,
then water (the materiall caufe) to make it cold. *Galen* *De vfu partium lib.8.cap.3.*
is of neither fide, for he doth not iudge it to be hot, nei-
ther doth he euer pronounce it to be cold: but by reafon
of his tenuity, apt to be altered either by heat or cold. As *De ortu & inter lib.2.& meteor.*
for moyfture, *Ariftotle* holds the Ayre to be moft moift, *4 cap.1 & 4.*
and water moft cold. *Galen* holds Water to bee moft *Gal.de fimpl.*
moyft. *Ariftotles* reafon for the predominance of moy- *med.fac.lib.12 cap.8. Item de*
fture in Ayre, is, becaufe it is moft hardly contained *Elementis.*
within his bounds : but the termination of things, pro-
ceedes from their oppofite qualities, as moyfture is terminated by drynefle, and drynefle by moyfture: and
drynefle doth as eafily terminate moyfture, as moyfture
                                        doth

doth terminate drynesse. And this difficulty of termina
tion in Ayre, may more properly bee ascribed to his
thinnesse and tenuity of parts, then to his moysture.
For dry exhalations will extend themselues as well as
moyst vapours; and as it is density that compacts, so it
is rarity that extends. Fire it selfe is hardly bounded, and

*Valesius cont.
lib. 1. cap 2.*

yet, not moyst. Those that would reconcile these differences, doe alledge that *Galen* speakes as a Physitian,
and meant that water was *humidissimum medicamen-
tum*: *Aristotle* as a Philosopher meant it to be *humidissimum elementum*. But this reconciliation giues little sa-
tisfaction. For how could water be *humidissimum me-
dicamentum*, if it were not *humidissimum elementum?*
We speake of the proper operation of water according
to his naturall qualitie, and not as it may worke by acci-

*De aere, aquis
& locis.*
*De morbis popu-
lar. lib. 2. sect. 2.*

dent. Thinnesse and leuitie are two other qualities of
simple water, which *Hippocrates* commends, and addes
this experiment in another place, that it is quickly hot,
and quickly cold. *Galen* addes another experiment in
the quicke boyling of Peasen or Beanes. And it is requi-
site that water should haue these qualities, in regard of
the manifold and necessarie vses of it, both for Man and
Beast, and Plants: insomuch, as there is no liuing for any

*Bruerinus de re
cibaria lib. 16.
cap. 7.*

creature, where there is no water. It was our first drinke
to quench our thirst, and to distribute our nourishment
as a *vehiculum*, which it doth by his tenuitie; and after
the inuention of Wine, it was mixed therewith, as *Vir-
gil* saith of *Bacchus, poculaque inuentis Acheloia miscuit
vuis*; where, by *Acheloia*, he meanes not onely the water

*Saturnal. lib. 5.
cap. 18.*

of the Riuer Achelous in Etolia, but all other waters, as
Macrobius proues out of *Aristophanes* and *Ephorus*. And
since the planting of Vineyards, seeing all Countries
could not beare Grapes, *Bacchus* also taught the world
to make *vinum è frugibus* with water, as *Diodorus
Siculus*

Siculus reports, from whence the Egyptians had their
Zithum and *Curmi*, the Spaniards their *Cerea*, the
Turkes their *Cowfet*, and wee our *Ale* and *Beere*; all
which are extracted out of Corne, by the purenesse and
tenuitie of water. By meanes whereof wee haue our
Brothes, Syrupes, Apozemes, &c. extracted with it, as
a fit menstruum to receiue the faculties of all medicaments and nourishments, especially the second qualities, and therefore it was anciently called *Panspermia* :
besides the manifold vses in washing, dying, &c. of
which I will not discourse farther. Leuitie is another
note of pure water, alledged by many, and serues well
to distinguish it from many mixed waters, whether wee
respect the weight of it, or the molestation which it
breedes in the bowels. This difference of weight is hardly discerned by ballance, both because simple waters
doe very little differ in this point, and also many mixt
waters, if they be onely infected with Spirits, and not
corporall substances, retaine the same proportion of
heauinesse with simple water: and also because it is hard
to haue great ballances so exact, as a small difference
may be discerned by them, yet *Agricola* reports that a
cotyle of the water of Pyrene and Euleus, did weigh a
dram lesse then the water of Euphrates, or Tigris, and
therefore the Kings of Persia vsed to drinke of it, and
held it in great account, as also the water of the Riuer
Coaspis. Thus much for the qualities which simple
water should haue; for such as it should not haue, I shall
not need to spend time in discourse, being either such as
the senses will discouer, ifit bee in taste, colour, smell,
or touch; or the effects,if it be purgatiue, vomitory, venomous, &c.

*Rerum anti-
quar. lib.4. c.2.*

Baccius lib.1.c 7

*De nat. eor. quæ
effl. è terra lib.1.
cap.15.*

*Langius Epist.
lib.1. Epist.32.*

Of the three originals of simple waters.

Baccius lib. 1.
cap. 3. 4. Agric:
de ortu & causis
subterr. lib. 1.
cap. 1. 2. 3. 4. 5.
6. 7. 8 9.
Solinander lib. 2.
cap. 1. & lib. 13
cap. 3.

NOw it followeth that we shew from whence these waters haue their originall, which is no other then of the mixt waters, sauing that the mixt waters doe participate with some minerals which are imbybed in them.

They haue three seuerall Originals: the one from moyst vapours congealed by cold in the ayre: the second from the earth; the third by percolation from the Sea.

For the first, it is certaine that our Springs and Riuers doe receiue great supply of waters from the Ayre, where vapours being congealed by cold, doe fall downe vpon the earth in raine, or snow, or haile, whereby the ground is not onely made fertile, but our Springs are reuiued, and our Riuers increased. As wee see the Rein and Danubius to swell more in summer then in winter, because then the snow which continually lyeth vpon the Alpes, doth melt by the heate of the sunne, and fils those Riuers, which haue their Originals from thence vp to the brinkes. Also we see daily after much raine, our small Lakes and Riuers to be very high. Also vpon much dryth our Springs faile vs in many places, which vpon store of raine doe supply vs againe with water. And this is the cause that in most parts of Africa, neere the Equinoctiall, where it raines little, they haue little water; and many times in two or three dayes iourney, can hardly finde to quench their thirsts and their Camels. *Leo Africanus* speakes of an Army wherein were many Camels, which in their marching, comming to a Riuer (perhaps it was but a Brooke) did drinke it dry. So that

we

we muſt acknowledge that the earth receiues much water this way. But how this ſhould ſerue the bowels of
the earth with ſufficiencie for the generations there,
and for perpetuall ſprings, is very doubtfull; whereas
Seneca ſaith that theſe waters doe not pierce aboue ten
foot into the earth : neither if there were paſſages for it
into the bowels of the earth, can the hundred part of it
be imployed this way, but is rudely conueyed by Riuers into the Sea. Wherefore although much water bee
yeelded to the ſuperficies of the earth by raine, and
ſnow, and haile from the ayre, yet not ſufficient to maintaine perpetuall Springs; ſeeing many times, and in many countries theſe aeriall ſupplies are wanting, or very
ſpare, and yet the Springs the ſame. Wherefore *Ariſto-*
tle his opinion, which attributes all to aeriall water and
vapours, from thence, is iuſtly reieƈted by *Agricola*, and
by our country-man Maſter *Lydiat*. So that wee muſt
finde out ſome other Originals, or elſe wee ſhall want
water for the manifold vſes the earth hath of it : from the
earth they make another originall of perpetuall Springs
and Riuers, ſeeing the firſt ſeemes to be ordained by nature onely for the irrigation of the ſuperficies of the
earth, which elſe would be in moſt places deſtitute of
water, where Springs are not, and ſo would be barren,
plants and trees wanting due moyſture for their nou-
riſhment. Wherefore for the perpetuitie of fountaines,
and for Subterraneall generations, which cannot proceede without water, they haue imagined a generation
of water within the earth; ſome holding that the earth it
ſelfe is conuerted into water, as elements are held to be
mutable and conuertable, the one into the other. But
neither fire will be conuerted into any other element, being ſuperiour vnto the reſt, and not to be maſtered by
cold, which onely muſt be the agent of the conuerſion

Quæſt. natur.
lib.3.cap.7.

2 Meteorol.
& 1 3.

De ortu & caſ-
ſis ſubt lib 3.c 6;
De orig. fonſ.
cap.1.

of it by condensation : neither will earth be conuerted
into water, for either heate or cold must conuert it. Heate
cannot doe it, although it rarifie and attenuate, both for
that it consumes moysture, and also because water is
cold, which it should not be, if it were made by heat; for

Aristotl.4. me-
teor. cap.10.&
vltimo.

euery naturall Agent workes to that end that it may
make the Patient like it selfe: and heate may conuert
earth into fume and dry exhalations, but not into water, for all water which is not eternall, is from cold;
likewise cold cannot conuert earth into water, because
cold doth congeale, condense, and congregate, and indu-
rate, and not dissolue and attenuate, &c. as wee see in
Amber and Gummes. Others will haue great receptacles of ayre within the earth, which flying vp and
downe, is congealed by the coldnesse of Rockes into

Valesius de sa-
cra philosoph.
passim.

water, to supply all wants. Others imagine huge Lakes
and Cisternes, primarilie framd in the earth, and sup-
plied with water, either from vapour or ayre, or from
the sea; which water either by agitation, by winds, or
by impulsion from the sea, or by compression of Rocks,
is eleuated to the Superficies of the earth: or els vapours
from thence, made by attenuation, either from the Sun
and Starres, or from Subterraneall fire kindled vpon
Sulpher and Bitumen; which vapours ascending to the
tops of mountaines, are there congealed into water by
the coldnesse of the Rockes; where there must be other
Cesternes or Castles in the ayre to feede the inferiour
Springs. These and such like deuices are produced for
the maintaining of their Originall; which as they are all
insufficient to afford such a proportion of water as is re-
quisite, so most of them are so improbable, and full of
desperate difficulties, as I am vnwilling to spend time
in the rehearsing of them, or their Authors, much more
vnwilling in confuting of them, to trouble my selfe, and

offend my Reader, onely the poynt of Subterraneall fire which hath taken deepeſt impreſſion in moſt mens mindes, I ſhall ſpeake of hereafter, when I come to ſhew the cauſes of the actuall heate of Springs. The third Originall is from the Sea, a ſufficient ſtorehouſe for all vſes, and whereunto the other two may be referred. For that which fals from the ayre, and that which is bred in the earth, doe proceed principally from the Sea. *Agricola* for feare of wanting water for his Springs, is contented to admit of all theſe Originals, although he relyeth leaſt vpon the Sea, becauſe he knowes not how to bring it vp to the heads of his fountaines, but is contented it ſhould ſerue for lower places neare the Sea coſte. As I remember I haue ſeene in Zeland at Weſtcapell, freſh Springs colated from the Sea, through bankes of ſand. But I make no doubt but that the Sea water may ſerue all other Springs and Riuers whatſoeuer, although both farre remote from the Sea, and high in ſituation. Neither ſhall we neede to flye for helpe to thoſe monſtrous conceits of Agitation, Compulſion, Compreſſion, Suction, Attraction by the Sunne, &c. But holding the ſacred Canon of the Scriptures, that all Riuers are from the Sea, &c. I perſwade my ſelfe, that there is a naturall reaſon for the eleuating of theſe waters vnto the heads of Fountaines and Riuers, although it hath not yet beene diſcouered. For thoſe opinions formerly mentioned will not hold water.

My conceit therefore is this, that as we ſee in *Siphunculis*, that water being put in at one end, will riſe vp in the other pipe, as high as the leuell of the water (whether by his waight, or by the correſpondence with his leuell, I will not diſpute) ſo it may be in the bowels of the earth; conſidering that the paſſages there are more firme to maintaine the continuitie of the water with the

De ortu & cauſis ſubter. lib. 1. cap. 5. & 9.

Eccleſiaſtes 2.

Sea, then any leaden pipes can be, being compassed on euery side with many Rockes: as we see in *Venis, fibris & commissuris saxorum.* Now although perhaps this water enters into the earth very deepe, yet the leuell of it must answer to the superficies of the Sea, which is likely to be as high as the superficies of the Land, seeing the natural place of waters is aboue the earth. And although neere the Coasts it bee depressed and lower then the Shoare, yet there is reason for that, becaufe it is terminated by the dry and solid body of the earth : as we see in a Cup or Bowle of water filled to the top, we may put in a great bulke of siluer in pieces, and yet it will not run ouer, but be heightened aboue the brims of the bowle. If this be euident in so small a proportion, we may imagine it to bee much more in the vast Ocean: and our Springs being commonly at the foot of hils, may well be inferiour to the Globe of the Sea, if any bee higher, they may perhaps be fed from raine and snow falling vpon the mountaines. But if *Iosephus a Costa*, his assertion bee true, that the Sea towards the Equinoctiall, is higher then towards the Poles, then the leuell of the Sea may bee much higher then the top of our highest hils, but this is a doubtfull assertion : yet I dare beleeue that if it were possible to immure a Spring without admission of ayre, which might breake the continuitie with the Sea, our Springs might be raised much higher. At Saint *Winifrids* Well in Flintshire, though there be no high land neere it, yet the Springs rise with such a violence, and so plentifully, that within a stones cast, it driues a Mill. It is likely that this Spring might be raised much higher. And whereas we see that Riuers doe run downewards to the Sea *per decline*, it doth not proue the Sea to be lower then the Land, but onely neere the shore where it is terminated, and in lieu of this it hath ſcope aſſigned it to fill vp the Globe, and ſo to be as high as the Land, if not higher. For if a meaſure ſhould bee taken of the Globe of the earth, it muſt be taken from the tops of the Mountaines, and from the higheſt of the Sea, and not from the Vallies, nor from the Sea-coaſts. This conceit of mine I was fearefull to publiſh, and therefore had written vnto Maſter *Brigges*, mine ancient friend, for his aduice in it, being a point wherein he was well ſtudied: but before my Letter came to Oxford, he was dead. But now I haue aduentured to publiſh it, to ſtir vp others to ſearch out the cauſes hereof, better then hath yet beene diſcouered. *Exors ipſe ſecandi, fungor vice cotis.*

Cap. 4.

Diuiſion of Minerall Waters. Minerals deſcribed. Their kindes recited. Of earth, ſimple and mixed. Whether it giue any medicinable qualitie to water. And ſo of the reſt in the following Chapters.

THus much of ſimple waters, and their originals, which may ſerue as *Polycletus* his rule to iudge mixed and infected waters by: as *Galen* in many places ſpeakes of an exact and ſound conſtitution of body, as a rule to diſcerne diſtempered and diſproportionated bodies. And thus much in explication of the *Genus*, in the definition of Minerall waters.

Now I come to Minerall Waters, and to the other part of the definition which wee call difference, &c. from Subterraneall Mynes by Imbibition.

Theſe Minerall waters are either ſimple or compound; ſimple, which partake but with ſome one Subterraneall Minerall; compound, which partake with moe

moe then one. And thefe waters partake with Minerals, either as they are confufed with them, or as they are perfectly mixed. Alfo thefe minerall waters, whether fimple or compound, are actually either hot or cold; the reafon whereof muft proceede from fome Subterraneall caufe, as fhall be fhewed hereafter.

Wherefore wee muft firft know the nature of thefe Subterraneall Minerals, and their generation, from whence Minerall waters receiue their difference, from common fimple water, before wee can iudge of the nature and qualitie of them, either Actuall or Potentiall.

By Minerals, we vnderftand all Inanimat perfect bodies, bred in Mynes within the bowels of the earth. I dare not vndertake to mufter thefe in due order by Dicotomyes, feeing neither *Agricola* nor *Fullopius*, nor *Libauius*, nor any other that I know, haue exactly done it, nor fatisfied either others or themfelues in it; and feeing there are diuers Minerals lately difcouered, and perhaps more may bee hereafter, which haue not beene knowne in former times, and therefore not mentioned; as *Calaem* in the Eaft Indies, *Rufma* and *terra ghetta* in Turkey, &c. Wherefore I will make bold to reckon them vp as they come to hand in feauen rankes.

The firft fhall be Earth.

Earth whether it be bred *ab exhalatione ficca refrigerata*, or *ex miftis per putredinem in fimum conuerfis*, or *ex lapidibus fole aut calore coctis & deinde aqua folutis, &c.* it is all inconcrete. As a little water gleweth it together in *Lutum*, fo a great deale diffolues it. But this is no proper diffolution, but onely a difioyning of parts by Imbybing the moyfture which conioyned them, into a greater proportion of water; for waters doe naturally runne together, like drops of quickfiluer, or melted mettall. Wherefore feeing the moyfture which is in

the

the earth, is not naturall, but aduentitious, not vnited essentially, but onely mixed accidentally, it may well be called an *inconcrete* substance, whose moysture is easily drawne from it, being readie to vnite it selfe with other moysture, and leaue his old body as it found it, that is, dust: yet so as that water retaines with it some taste or qualitie which it receiued from the earth. This dust is neither a simple body, as Elements are, nor permanent in one and the same kinde : but as it participates with *animales vegetables*, and minerals, so it is apt to bee transmuted into any of them, being both Mother and Nurse to all terrestriall bodies.

Agric.de nat.
fossil. lib. 1.
cap.4.

Simple earth, if it be not mixed with other substances, is dry and cold, and Astringent. But if it bee mixed, as commonly it is, it altereth his qualitie according to the mixture. Mine intent is to write of it as it is simple, and so of the rest.

Simple earth yeelds but a muddie water of it selfe, and of no vse in Physicke, but if it be mixed with other Minerals, it makes the water to participate with the quality of those Minerals also. As if it be mixed with niter, as in Fullers earth and Marle, it makes the water abstergent like Soape. If with Allum or Copperesse, astringent and more desiccatiue, as in all sorts of Boles. If with Bitumen, fattie and Vnctious, as in Turfe and Peate, &c. We haue diuers examples of all sorts. The Bath of Mount Othon in Italy is full of clay, which is a kinde of Bole. The Bath Caldaria, full of Ocre. The Bath of Saint *Peter* full of a yellow earth, tincted belike with some other Minerals. Wherefore these are to bee iudged of according to the seuerall Minerals which they containe. But seeing earth it selfe makes little impression into water, neither doe wee make any Physicall vse of waters, which containe nothing but earth, I neede not spend any time about them.　　D　　**CAP.**

Baccius lib.5.
cap. 1.

CAP. 5.
Of Stone.

De metallis cap. 6.

THe second shall be Stone. Stone is another Minerall substance, concrete and more heauie then earth, and our Minerall men confound themselues much in the definition of it. Wherefore *Fallopius* implores the helpe of *Marcus Antonius Iunica* about it, as one of the most difficult points in Philosophie: but in the end, defines it by his want of dissolution, either by heate or moysture. And whereas it is manifest that some Stones will melt, he imputes it to the admixture of some mettall, among which he receiueth glasse. Others define it by his hardnesse, wherein commonly it goeth beyond other Minerals. But you shall haue some stones softer then some of those, and therefore the definition is not good. Others by this, that being broken or calcind, they will not bee consolidated againe into their former consistence or shape. But for breaking, the reason of that, is want of fusion; for without fusion or ignition, which is a kinde or degree of fusion; Mettals also being broken, will not be consolidated into the same Masse againe. And there is no more difference in nature or essence, betweene a whole stone and a broken, then there is betweene a masse of Mettall, and the powder or filings of the same. As for calcination, other minerals may bee so far calcind, and brought to a Crocus by fire, as they will be irreducible, therefore this is not p oper to stone. Wherefore I am of *Fallopius* his opinion in this point, and the rather because otherwise there would seeme to be a species in nature wanting, if there were not Minerall Species wanting, dissolut on by heate or moysture, as well as there are, hauing such dissolution. And this *vacuum* which

nature abhorres, is not onely to be vnderftood of a lo-
call vacuitie, but alfo of a want of fuch fpecies as are in
natures power to produce, for the ornament of the
world. For if it be a naturall paffion to be diffolued, it is
likewife a naturall paffion not to bee diffolued : and if
fome things will bee diffolued both by heate and moyfture, as Salts, why fhould there not be other fubftances
which will be diffolued by neither of them. And this
muft be ftone, for nature affords none other. Moreouer
according to *Ariftotle: Quæ concreuerunt a frigido & a
calido, a nullo iftorum diffoluuntur.* Of this kinde are
Stones which could neuer attaine to fuch puritie as many of them haue, if they were not congealed by heate as
well as by cold. Alfo vnder what fpecies fhall we comprehend, Diamonds, Talcum, *Magnetis, Glymmer,
Katzenfilber, pyrimachus, amiantus, alumen plumofum,
faxum arenarium mortuum, &c.* if not among Stones?
yet thefe are confeffed to be inuincible by fire or water.
Alfo all pretious Stones, the more noble and pretious
they are, the more they refift diffolution either by fire
or water : for this qualitie fheweth the perfection of
their mixture. True it is that fome ftones wilbe diffolued
by fire or water, and therefore *Pliny* and *Agricola* di-
uide Stones into fufible and infufible : but this is in regard of other fubftances bred in the ftone; which if it be
Metall, the fufion will be Metallin: If Niter or meane
Minerals, it will bee vitrificatorie. As *Pliny* reports of
the inuention of Glaffe by certaine Merchants, who mel-
ting Niter vpon the fand in Siria, where with clods of
Niter they had made a furnace for their neceffary vfe;
found that cleere mettall which we ca'l glaffe, *Ecce li-
quato nitro cum arenis vifi funt riui fluxiffe nobilis liquoris.*

If Sulphur, as in *pyrite,* it will likewife melt and ftrike
fire.

fire. And whereas the ſtriking of fire out of a flint or py-
rits, is held by all men to proceede from the kindling of
ayre, by the colliſion of two hard ſubſtances together,
they are miſtaken. For then Diamonds, Chryſtall
Glaſſe, &c. ſhould ſtrike fire as well as flints, but it is the
Sulpher contained in them: And G. *Fabricius* in his ob-
ſeruations, although hee obſerues not the reaſon of this
fire, yet he confeſſeth that out of any Pyrites *è quo excu-
titur ignis, etiam excoquitur ſulphur. Pliny* giues the
reaſon of the name, *quia ineſt ignis illi.* The like we obſerue in Indian Canes, and ſome Woods that are vnctuous, and full of oyle, which will yeeld fire by frication,
or colliſion, not by kindling the ayre thereby, but the
inflamable oyle in them. If other concrete iuyce bee
mixed with ſtone, as Salt, Allum, Vitrioll, &c. it makes
them to relent in water or moyſt ayre; and theſe ſtones
are neuer good to build withall. But let vs take ſtone as

*Eraſtus diſput.
part. 2. pag. 205.*

it is in it ſelfe, without the admixture of other Minerals,
and we ſhall find it to be indiſſoluble and inuincible, either by fire or water. Metallurgians and Refyners may
make vſe of this for their Shirbs, Tiegles, Hearths,
Teſts, &c. Stones are naturally dry and cold, and aſtringent like a concrete earth.

Simple Stones which haue no other Minerals mixed
with them, and are come to their perfection, being indiſſoluble, either by fire or water, can yeeld no qualitie or vertue to Bathes, and therefore hee that ſeekes to
draw any vertue from ſtone into water, doth *lapidem
lauare,* that is, labour in vaine. But by reaſon of admixtures, they may, or whileſt they are *ſucco lapideſcente,*
before they are concreted. For it it be certaine that mettals may yeeld vertue to Bathes, being alike indiſſoluble
by water, there is no reaſon but Stones alſo may. *Fullopius* is aguinſt it in both, but contradicted by *Iulius
Cæſar*

Cæsar, Claudius, and diuers others; yet hee confesseth that *Balneum montis Grotti,* hath *Gypsum* : and *Gesner* affirmes the same of the Baths of Eugesta. Also he findes *ramenta marmoris in Balneo Corsenæ & Agnano,* but he iudgeth that they receiue no qualitie but from the iuyce, and I doubt not but he is in the right. And for *succus lapidescens,* we haue many examples in *Agro Pisano & Lucensi* in Italy, in Auernia in France, where this iuyce is so plentifully brought by a cleare Spring, that after it is congealed, the people digge the stones, and haue made a great bridge of them. Also neere Vienna in Sauoy, in a village called Giaret, is a cleare fountaine which turnes to stones as hard as flints: *Pliny* makes mention of the like Springs in Eubea, which are hot: and *Vitruuius* of the like at Hieropolis in Phrygia: Also *Iosephus a Costa* of the like hot Springs in Guaniauilica in Peru, which turnes to stone, whereof they build their houses. *Anthonio de Herreza, cap.* 20. tels of the same Spring at Guainia velica, which turnes to stone as it ariseth, and kils those that drinke of it. Also this *Succus lapidescens* is obserued in the Bathes of Apono, where it is conuerted into stone vpon the sides of the Bath. Also in the Bath of Rancolani, where this iuyce is not confused, but perfectly mixed with the water, & being imbybed by plants, it hardens them like stone. *Bacius* tels vs of a Caue by Fileg in Transiluania, which turnes water into stone. The like is found at Glainstaynes in Scotland, as *Hector Boetius* reports. In England also we haue many fountaines which turne wood into stone: which must be by reason of this *succus lapidescens* mixed with the water. Corall also being a plant, and nourished with this iuyce, turnes to a stone: so doth the seede of Lithospermon or Gromell. Thus much of stone.

In ingressu ad infirmos p. 373. *Venustus in consilio pro Petro Picardo. Baccius etym*

*Bac- Lib.6.c.*14

D 3 C A P.

Cap. 6.

Of Bitumen. His kindes, qualities. Of Camfor in par-
ticular. That Bitumen is predominant in the waters of
Bathe.

NExt I come to thofe Minerals which we call *Bitu-*
mina, which are Minerall fubftances that burne
and wafte in the fire without metallin fufion, or ingreffion. The greateft affinitie they haue, is with Sulphur:
but this hath ingreffion into mettall, and Bitumen hath
none. Of this kinde fome are folid, and fome liquid. Solid, as *Succinum, gagates, ambra, camphora, terra am-*
pelitis, Lithanthrax, fiue carbofoffilis, &c. Liquid, as
petroleum and *naphtha.* All thefe are great fuels to
fire, efpecially thofe that are liquid, which are thought
to draw fire vnto them, if it be within their *effluuium:*
So *Pliny* reports that *Medea* burnt *Creufa* by anoynting
her Garland with Naphtha: and *Strabo* tels how *Alex-*
anders Bath-mafter, *Athenophanes,* had almoft burnt
Stephanus, a boy in the Bath, by fprinkling Naphtha
vpon him, if it had not beene fuddenly quenched. And
this is that iuyce or thicke water which *Plato* in *Timeo*
reckons among fires, and which the Egyptians vfed in
their facrifices, and was hidden by the Iewifh Priefts
in a dry pit for 70. yeares, and afterwards found by
Nehemias.

Machab. 2. 1.

But whereas it is a common receiued opinion, that
fome of thefe *Bitumina* will burne in water, I cannot beleeue it: although *Plynie* and *Agricola,* and moft that
haue written fince, out of them doe auerre it, and bring
arguments and examples to proue it. For although water were a fewell to fire, as oyle is, yet there can bee no
fire without ayre, and water excludes ayre: and fo doth

oyle, if the fire be beneath it, and couered with it. As
for their arguments, they fay that Bitumen being be-
fprinckled with water, burnes more, and therefore water is a fewell to it: as we fee that Smiths caft water vpon their Sea-cole in their Forges : but the reafon of this
is becaufe their Coale being fmall like duft, the water
makes it to cake and bake togerher, where otherwife
the blaft would blow it away: alfo it hinders the quicke
burning of it, and fo makes it continue the longer : fo in
a *Vulcano* after raine, they finde the fire to burne more,
when the Bitumen is fmall, and in duft. Although this
may be a reafon of it, that the Lyme which hath there
beene calcined, being by raine diffolued, increafeth the
fire. And whereas they fay that water will kindle Bitumen, and quench Sulphur, it is not fo: neither doth their
example of Wilde-fire proue it. For in Wild fire, befides Bitumen and Campher, there is quicke Lyme,
which by reafon of the fodaine diffolution of his Salt,
by the affufion of water, is apt to kindle any combuftible matter; not by reafon of any Bitumen in the Lyme,
as fome imagine, nor of any *Empyreuma* which the fire
hath left in it, as *Tracaftorius* thinks : for, how can *De fympathi &*
there be any Bitumen left in the Lyme (if there were a- *antipath.cap.*10,
ny at firft) after calcination : the fire would haue con-
fumed that before any thing elfe. And as for any *Empyreuma*, it is certaine that the more any thing is burnt,
although the fire leaue an aduftion in it, the leffe apt
it is to burne againe, efpecial y being burnt and calcind
ad calcem aut cineres, where all the combuftible matter
is fpent. Wherefore it muft needs bee by the violent
motion which is in the fuddaine diffolution of the falt
in it, as appeares by the crackling it makes : *Et ex motu
fit calor.* The like we obferue in *Pyrite fterili* whereof
they make Vitrioll, which being broken and laid vp

in

in heapes, and moyftned with water, will gather heat, and kindle any combuftible matter put to it. The like alfo we finde in Allum myne, &c. where thofe minerall iuyces being concrete in the Myne, when they come to fuddaine diffolution doe grow hot, and will kindle fuell. And as for the example of the falt Lake whereof *Agricola* writes, betweene *Strapela* and *Seburgh,* which burnes the fifhermens nets if they be put neare the bottome: and of the like *Sputa,* in *Media,* mentioned by *Strabo,* which burnes clothes put into it: I take that to be by reafon of the corrofiue quality of the falt which frets them, being ftronger neare the bottome; and not from Bitumen, as *Agricola* thinks. The like I iudge of the Lake by *Denftadt* in *Turingia.* And it is very probable that falt being heauier then water, wilbe moft towards the bottome: as it is reported of the fountaine *Achilleus* in *Mileto,* whofe water is very fweet and frefh aboue, and very falt towards the bottome. So is the water of *Agnano* in *Italy,* as M. *Sandys* reports in his trauels. And the more heauy and terreftriall any falt is, the more corrofiue it is: and fo contrariwife, the more corrofiue, the more heauy. *Ariftotle* affirmes the fea water to be more falt at the bottome then aboue: and fo doth *Pliny,* who likewife makes mention of the Lake *Afcanius* in *Chalcide,* whofe top is fweet, and bottome nitrous. *Baccius* writes the like of a Well neare *Toletum* in *Spaine,* the water whereof is fweet aboue, and corrofiue beneath: which he iudgeth to be from Quickfiluer. *Fullopius* is alfo of opinion, that Bitumen doth not only burne in water, but is nourifhed by water, becaufe it makes the fire to laft longer. But I haue fhewed the reafon of that before. And for the burning in water, he fhould haue faid vpon the water; for there it wil burn as long as it fwimmeth; but dip it vnder the water, and it is prefently extinguifhed.

De nat. cor. q. efflu. e terra. l 4. c. 22.

Meteor. 2.

Lib 6. c. 111

De Thermis. c. 5.

And whereas fome report that Queene *Anne* of bleffed memory, being in our Kings Bath, there arofe a flame of fire like a candle from the bottome of the Bath to the top neare vnto her, they muft giue mee leaue not to beleeue it, but rather to thinke they were miftaken : for, I am not bound to beleeue any thing againft reafon, which God hath giuen mee to bee my guide. It might haue beene fome bubble of winde which is frequent in our Bathes, or fome Bitumious matter not diffolued in the water did arife, and being at the top, diffolue it felfe vpon the furface in the forme of a circle: but it could not be kindled. And if it might bee kindled in the water (which were impoffible) yet in all likelyhood it would haue burnt better aboue the water then within it, and not be prefently extinct, as they report. Thefe *Bitumiana* (excepting Camfer) are potentially hot and dry in the fecond or third degree ; but concerning Camfer there are two doubts. Firft, whether it be a Bitumen or a Gum. Secondly, whether it be hot or cold. The Arabians affirme it to bee the Gum of a huge tree with white leaues, vnder whofe fhadow many wild beafts may lie : and that after earthquakes there is great plenty found; that it is in quality cold and dry in the third degree ; fome late writers follow them in their opinion of a Gum, as *Mathiolus*, *Amatus Lufitanus*, *Garrius ab horto*, &c. *Platearius* holds it to bee the iuyce of an herbe. But we muft confider that they make two forts of Camfer, the one of *Borneo*, the other of *Chyna*. For that of *Chyna* they confeffe it is adulterated with Bitumen : and that is the only Camfer in vfe with vs. But that of *Borneo* to bee a fimple Gum, and that a pound of this is valued as deare as an hundred pound weight of the other. So that all the doubt lyeth in this Camfer of *Borneo* ; which whether it be a Gum

Serapio de fimp. med. c.344. Avicen.lib 1: tract.1.c.2.Item l.2.tract.2 cap. 133. Item de med.cordial. tract.2.cap.3.

E   or

or no, is ſtill in controuerſie. For the Arabians not tra-
ding into thoſe parts, had the notice hereof only from
others, as *Serapio* and *Avicen* doe confeſſe: and *Amatus*
Luſitanus ſaith that the inhabitans will not ſuffer ſtran-
gers to come aſhore to ſee it. So as we haue beene kept
in ignorance a long time from the true knowledge of it.
And *Garrius ab horto* tels vs, that all his knowledge of
it, is but by relation: himſelfe not being able to trauell
to ſee it; partly by reaſon of his age, and partly for his
continuall imployment about the Viceroy. Only *Ed-*
uardus Barbeſa reports that he did ſee the place in *Bor-*
neo, and found it to be of a minerall nature. I procured
ſome of that Camfer to be brought from thence by my
worthy friend Captaine *Beſt,* but whether it be a Gum
or a Bitumen, by the view I cannot diſcerne. But if it be a
Gum, why ſhould it abound more after earthquakes?
and why ſhould it burne and not diſſolue in water?
No Gums will burne, and all Gums will diſſolue in water: and earthquakes make no trees fruitfull, but may
caſt forth minerals. That there is a naturall Bitumious
Camphire, I make no doubt: and *Agricola* proues it
ſufficiently: And the Bath in *Romandiola* neare *Rhegi-*
um ſhewes it. Alſo the Well by *Muntzbach* where *Ta-*
berni montani ſaith there is mineral Camphir. *Averroes*
ſaith it is *affinis Bitumini.*

Now for the qualities of it, the moſt generall and tru-
eſt opinion is, that it is cold and dry. *Matthiolus* iudgeth it to be hot for three eſpeciall reaſons. Firſt, becauſe
it burnes, and is a great fuell to fire. If this argument
bee good, then flax, and ſtraw, and paper, and touch-
wood, and ſpunck ſhould be hot, for they are apt fuels
to fire. Secondly, becauſe it is *odorata,* and hee holds
all *odorata* to be *calida*: *Galen* is of another opinion,
and holds the iudgement of ſimples by ſauour to be vn-

In Dioſcoridem
Cap.de maſtich.

Lib.1 Cap.9.

De nat.foſſil.
lib.4.cap.2.

Theſaur. aquar.
lib.1.cap.2.

Comment.in Di-
oſc. et Epiſt.l.3.
Thaddeo Nemi-
co.

De ſimpl. med.
facult.l.4.c.22.

certaine. And as for Campher, *Galen* knew it not. A-
vicen saith expreſſely of Campher, that although it bee *Lib.i.traff.1.c.2*
odorata, yet it is *frigida*. And if *Matthiolus* his reaſon
were good, then Roſes, and Violets, and Vinegar
ſhould be hot; for they are *odorata*. It is true that all
ſauors ariſe from heat, as *Galen* ſaith, and all compounded bodies haue ſome hot parts: but wee ſpeake of the
predominancy in the ſubiect. Thirdly, becauſe it bytes
the tongue. So doth iuyce of Limons, and Barberies,
and Vinegar, &c. and yet they are cold. Wherefore I
conclude our Campher to be a Bitumen, and in quality
cold and dry; and of very ſubtill parts. Theſe *Bitumina*
being vnctuous and oylie, diſſolue not of themſelues in
water, without the helpe of ſome minerall iuyce, but
may be confuſed with it. And wee haue many fountaines and lakes which participate with them. In Shrop-
ſhire at *Pitchford* is a ſpring that caſteth forth Bitumen
ſwimming vpon the water. The like we read of in *A-
vernia* in *France* betweene *Claremond* and *Monferan*,
where the people gather it for their vſes. In *Italy* there
are many fountaines yeelding Bitumen, at *Maianum*,
and *Saſſoli*, and *Salſa*, and *Herculanum* at the foot of the
mountaine *Veſuvium*, at *Baia*, and alſo at the cape of S.
Helena, and in the Iſle of *Woolfs* there are fountaines of
pitchie Bitumen, which are vſed to pitch ropes and
tackling, as *Ioſephus à coſta* reports. And we haue that *Bellonius de*
famous lake *Aſphaltites* in *Iudæa* ſo full of Bitumen, that *Naphtha c.78*
it hardly ſuffers any thing to ſincke in it. The riuer *Li-
paris* in *Cilicia* by reaſon of a ſpring neare *Solos* is ſo *Agric. de nat.*
full of liquid Bitumen, as they which ſwim or waſh in *eor.quæ efflu. è*
it ſeeme to be anointed with oyle. Alſo there are Bitu- *terra.l: 1.c.7.*
mious ſprings in *Saxony* at *Bruno*, in *Sweuia*, the lake
Tegera at *Gerſedorf* vnder the mount *Iurat*; In *Aſia*
by *Tralleis* and *Niſſa*. Alſo in the Weſt Indies there

are many found which they put to vfe for fhipping.
And this Bitumen is the chiefe ingredient in our Baths
at Bath in Somerfetfhire, although dilated with much
Niter, which makes the folution the better, and the water more cleare.   That Bitumen is predominant in thefe
our Baths, may bee proued by the effects, becaufe wee
finde them exceedingly to comfor the nerues, fupple the
ioynts, dry vp rheumes, cure Palfies, and Contractions,
being diftinctly vfed, tinct filuer into the colour of gold,
&c.   Alfo by the Bitumeous fauour of them, and by
the neighbourhood of Cole mines in thofe parts.   All
which doe argue Bitumen to abound in them.   And
whereas Doctor *William Turner* in his treatife of thefe
Baths, thinketh Brimftone to bee the chiefe minerall,
and Copper next ; I am out of his opinion.   The actuall
heat is no argument of Brimftone, as fhall bee fhewed
when I come to that point : nether doth the fauour be-
wray it.   But his reafon for Copper is very weake.   He
found a Marchefit vpon one of the hils, which hee
thought to hould Copper.   But Marchefits although
they fhew yellow, yet they feldome hold Copper, or
any other metall.   But his difcourfe hath perfwaded
Iohn Bauhinus to publifh it confidently to the world.
I fhall haue occafion to fpeake more of this hereafter.
And thus much of *Bitumina*,

De thermis Boll.
l.3:c.61.

Cap. 7.

Of Minerall iuyces concrete : called by the Alchimifts, Salts. The foure principall forts of them ; Salt, Niter, Allum, Vitrioll.

A Fourth fort of minerals are concrete iuyces which are minerall fubftances diffoluble in water. Thefe the Alchimifts call Salts, and are the meanes of communicating all other minerals with water. For as water is apt to diffolue and extract vegetables, fo are thefe concrete iuyces apt to diffolue and extract minerall fubftances. And although they are found fometimes liquid being diffolued by moifture : yet we call them concrete, becaufe they will be concrete when the aduentitious moifture is remoued. Our minerall Authors doe make many forts of thefe according to the feuerall minerals which they imbibe : but in truth they may bee all reduced to foure heads ; Salt, Niter, Allum, and Vitrioll. And each of thefe hath diuers fpecies, as *Geber* and *Cafulpinus* fay of Salt, *quot genera calcium, tot genera falium.* Concerning Vitrioll there may bee fome doubt whether it be a diftinct fpecies from Allum, and and haue receiued only fome tincture from Copper, or Iron, or from fome of their brood, which are called excrements. For in diftilling oyle of Vitrioll, the lute wherewith the glaffes are ioyned, will yeeld perfect Allum. And Vitrioll being boyld arifeth in balls as Allum doth, and fhoots like Allum *in globos* ; as Salt doth *in tefferas*, and Niter *in ftirias.* Among thefe concrete iuyces *Agricola* reckons Sulphur, Bitumen, Auripigmentum, Sandaracha, Chrifocola, Erugo, Myfi, Sori, Melanteria, &c. But if wee examine them aright, wee fhall finde, that either they are not diffoluble in water as

Libauius in Syntagm.p.221.

Cafalpinus de metallis c.3.l.1.

E 3   concrete

concrete iuyces fhould be, or they are fome of thofe iuyces tincted or incorporated with other mineralls. All thefe minerall iuyces are accounted hot, and dry, and aftringent, and detergent, fome more, fome leffe: and we take it fo vpon truft. But this point requires further confideration and diftinction.

Salt is aftringent, detergent, purging, difperfing, repelling, attenuating, makes an efcar, and preferues from putrifaction, as *Diofcorides* informes vs, and *Galen* confirmes the fame, adding that it is hot. But we muft vnderftand *Galen* with this limitation, *lib. 6. cap. 30.* That the more it is deterfory, the leffe it is aftringent. And all aftringent things are cold, as hee auoucheth, *lib. 4. cap. 6. Acida, acerba, & aftringentia omnia frigida.* Now if falt be aftringent, it muft bee cold by *Galens* owne rule, and it is not enough to fay it hath warme parts in it, but being an vniforme fubftance, wee muft determine of it *ex prædominio.* Alfo *Galen lib. 1. Symp. cap. 4.* comparing pure water with fea water, feemes to affirme that fea water, before it haue recciued any great aduentitious cold, may coole our bodyes. And fo this place is vnderftood by *Anthonius Maria Venuftus in confilio pro Petro Picardo,* The repelling quality, and the making an efcar, and the preferuing from putrifaction, are arguments of drineffe, and not of heat. For as heat and moyfture are principall agents in generation and corruption; fo cold and drineffe in preferuation. Alfo I fhould impute the purgatiue and deterforie qualities in falt rather to the tenuity of parts, and the ftimulation which it hath from thence, then to any heat; for then as *Sennertus* faith, all hot things fhould purge; *Inftit. lib. 5. part. 1. cap. 11. Valeriala in Gal. de conftit. artis pag. 447.* And *Mefne Canon. vniverfal. cap. 1.* reiects all elementary qualities, temperaments, fimilitudes, or contrarieties

Diofc. l. 5. c. 84.
De fimpl. med.
facult. l. 4. c. 20.
& l. 11, c. 50.

contrarieties of fubftances, &c. in purging medicines.
Alfo Tamarinds, Myrabolans, and Antimony doe
purge, and yet are cold, *Venuſtus pag.* 1 3 2. But the purgatiue faculty of medicines is from ftimulation of the
expulfiue faculty of the ftomach and guts, and not from
attraction by heat of peculiar humors, as hath beene
imagined. Heat may ferue as an inftrument to actuate
ftimulation, as cold doth dull and benumbe all faculties, but neither heat nor cold are principall agents in
this worke. And whereas Reubarb is thought to
purge coller only, Sene and Polipody melancholy, A-
garick phlegme, &c. becaufe wee fee the excrements
tincted with the fame colors, it is a deceit : for thefe purgations doe colour humors in that manner. Yet I doe
not deny a diftinction to be made of purgations in o-
ther refpects. And our ancient Phyfitians through
long experience haue found out the right vfe of purging medicines, and their true diftinctions for feuerall
vfes for mens bodies : as that fome doe purge groffe
humors, and fome thin, fome are ftrong, and fome
weake : fome are comfortable to the ftomach, or liuer,
or fpleen, &c. and fome hurtfull to fome of thofe parts :
fome are too hot in fome cafes, and fome temperate,&c.
But they haue not difcouered the true caufe of this
purging quality : fome attributing it to a celeftiall influence, fome to a hidden quality, which is as much as if
they had faid nothing : fome to a Sympathy, Antipa-
thy, &c. For my part I hold the purgatiue quality of
mixt bodies to lie principally in the terreftriall part of
them, which is their falt : and therefore the Chymifts
vfe to acuate their purging extracts with their proper
falts. It were much better if they could make their
falts without calcination : for then they fhould retaine
the taft of the Simples, which lyeth in the falt, and
much

much other vertue which the fire confumes in calcination. And I am likewife of opinion, that as their purgatiue qualitie lyeth in the Salt, fo it workes by Stimulation, a qualitie moft proper to Salt, whereby it furthers
all generations, &c.

Niter doth dry and attenuate more then falt, and although it hath not fo much aftriction as Salt is faid to
haue, yet it feemes to coole more then Salt, perhaps becaufe it is of thinner parts, and penetrates more, and
that is the reafon that it ferues better for the diffolution
of Mettals. In phyficke we finde our Sal nitrum (which
is a kinde of it) to coole the body mightily, and therefore vfed in Iuleps : Allum and Vitriol are much alike,
but that Vitriol hath a garbe from Copper or yron.
Thefe are very aftringent, and without doubt cold,
whatfoeuer hath beene held of them.   The waters or
phlegmes diftilled from them doe exceedingly coole in

In peftis Alexic. Dariot de praparat.med. Tract.2.cap.23 24.

Iuleps, as *Quercitan* and *Claudius Dariot* haue obferued, and we alfo by daily experience doe finde true : by
reafon of the intenfe aciditie they haue, being diftilled
from their Terreftriall parts. Alfo thofe *acidula* which
the Germans call Saurbrun, proceeding from thefe iuyces, are much vfed to quench the heate of feuers. It may
be obiected, that they are Corrofiues, and will eate into
mettall, and therefore muft bee hot.   But by the fame
reafon, the iuyces of Limmons, Barberies, Howfleeke,
&c. fhould be hot, for they will carue iron. To bite and
eate as a Corofiue, are not arguments of heate, but of
piercing: Wherefore *Hippocrates* faith, *Frigus vlceri-
bus mordax*, and *frigus eft principium deftructiuum,vt
calor generatiunm*. And therefore it is more probable
that thefe corrofiues are more cold then hot. Thefe two
minerall iuyces are not fo readily diffolued in water, as
the other two, and will be more eafily precipitated by

any oppofite fubftance that is more familiar to water. I omit the feuerall forts of thefe concrete iuyces and their admixtures with other minerals, as impertinent to my purpofe : wherefore I will fhew fome examples of each of them in naturall Springs.

For falt Springs, *Iofephus a Cofta* tels vs of a rare Spring at a farme neere Cufco in Peru, which as it runs, turnes into very white Salt, without any fire or Art, in great abundance. In Germany are many falt fountaines, at Luneburg, Stafford, Saltzburg, Aldondorg, Halftat, &c. In Italy, *in agro Volaterano*, &c. In Cicily, at Solinantia, is a falt Well which is hot; and fo are the Pegafæi fonts in Caria. Alfo the fountaine by Medon in Træfen is both falt and hot. Our Wiches in Chefhire are well knowne. There are alfo Riuers of falt water by the Cafpian ftreights, and in Spaine, and Caria, and in Bactria, Ochus and Oxus. Alfo there are falt Lakes, as the Tarentin Lakes in Italy, the Lake betweene Strapela and Seburg (mentioned before) In Germany three Lakes, in Cicily, and befides an infinite number in other Countries, the Lake of Lakes, the Sea. All which receiue their faltneffe from Mynes of falt in the earth, which are very frequent and huge in bigneffe, as may appeare by the Rocks of Salt in Bohemia, in monte Carpato, in Polonia, within two miles of Cracouia, in Heluetia, and Rhetia, where they haue no other falt but from the Rocke. As alfo by the Cafpian Straights, are great Rocks of Salt. But *Marcus Paulus Venetus*, tels vs of a Rocke or Mountaine of Salt in *Thaican*, able to furnifh all the World with Salt. So that it is no maruaile that the Sea is falt, feeing it pierceth into the bowels of the earth, and difcouereth many great Rockes of Salt which diffolue in it. And this is the true caufe of the faltneffe of the Sea. And confidering the

Lib. 3.

F　　　　great

great vſe of Salt, both for other vſes, and for generations, nature hath prouided enough of it, eſpecially in
the Sea, which is more fruitfull in that reſpect, then the
Land. VVherefore *Venus* was called Αλιγένη : *Eſt Venus
orta Mari.*

Niter is ſeldome found in Bathes alone, but mixt with
other minerals, which it diſſolues, and infects the water withall. Yet we reade of a nitrous Lake called Le-
tis, neere Caleſtria in Macedonia, where they vſe to
make Niter, and vent it to all parts. So they doe at the
Nitrarie in Egypt. Alſo the Lake Arethuſa in Armenia,
is full of Niter. At Menis in Phrygia is a Spring of nitrous water which is hot: alſo in Leonte is a hot nitrous
Spring. *Bellonius* makes mention of a Nitrous fountaine
neere Belba, and of abundance of Niter vpon a Plaine
neere thereunto, which ſeemes to be that which *Pliny*
cals Halmiraga. But he denieth that there is any Mine
of Niter vnder the earth, but that all is bred out of the
Soyle as an *effloreſcens* of the earth : *Baccius* ſaith the
ſame of Salt-Peter. *Agricola* ſaith, that as the true Niter is gathered vpon the Playnes of Media aboue the
earth, ſo is Salt-peter found aboue the earth in many
places of Saxony : That, Niter is gathered vpon the
Plaines of Media, are *Plinys* owne words. *Exiguum fit
apud Medos caneſcentibus ſiccitate conuallibus.* So that it
ſeemeth, his opinion was, that Niter is not bred in a
Myne vnder the earth, but in the earth it ſelfe, as the
chieſe fatneſſe it hath to further generations. And ſeeing earth is the mother of all Terreſtriall bodies, it is
not left vnfurniſhed with thoſe minerall iuyces, nor
ought elſe that is requiſite for the production of ſpecies:
It hath beene obſerued by ſome, that nitrous water is
the beſt ſoyle for ground, and brings all Plants to perfection farre ſooner then any other dung, and therefore
the

*Obſeruat.l·3:
c.76,77·*

Lib.5.c.7.

Lib.3 1.c.13.

the Egyptians water their Coleworts with Nitrous water, *Nitrofa viridis braßica fiet aqua.* Our Salt-peter Martial,
men doe finde, that if any fat earth bee couered from
raine and fun, fo as it fpendeth not his ftrength in producing of Hearbs or Graffe, it will breede plenty of
Salt-peter, otherwife it will yeeld none. The difference
betweene Salt peter and the ancient Niter, appeares in
this, that a pound of Niter being burnt, will leaue foure
ounces of afhes; Salt-peter will leaue none. Salt-peter is
actually fo cold, as being diffolued in water, it is vfed in
Rome and Naples to coole their Wine, and doth it as
well as yce or fnow. Alfo we vfe it inwardly in cooling
Iuleps, and therefore it feemes alfo to bee potentially
cold, as *Bellonius* iudgeth.

Now I come to Allum (*Indignum vox ipfa iubet re-
nouare dolorem*) the greateft debitor I haue, and I the
beft benefactor to it, as fhall appeare when I fhall think
fit to publifh the Artifice thereof. In Illua, a myle from
Rio, is an Allum fountaine: alfo there are diuers in A-
gro Senenfi, Volaterano Lucenfie, in Italy, *Balneum de
villa* is full of Allum: and with vs in Shropfhire at O-
kenyate, are Allum fprings, whereof the Dyers of
Shrewesbury make vfe in ftead of Allum. As for allum
Mynes, they are frequent almoft in all Countries, but
the chiefeft that are wrought, are at Capfylar in Thracia, at Tolpha neere Ciuita Vectia in Italy, at Commataw by Auffig in Germany, and with vs in Yorkefhire,
In Ireland there haue beene Allum workes neere to Ar-
magh, as *Thurmifer* reports: alfo at Metelin in Spayne.
at Mazaron neere Garthage, at Hellefpont, Maffa, Mon-
trond, Piambin, Volterra, Campiglia, &c. as *Beringac-* Pyrotechnia
cio Sienefe reports. Alfo there are diuers earths yeelding l.2.c.6.
allum, as at Guyder in Carnaruanfhire, at Camfurt in
Dorfetfhire, and in the Ile of Wyght. But I will contract

my felfe for Allum, and come to Vitriol.

Vitriol, as I haue faid before, doth participate much
with Allum in the manner of fhooting or roching,
which is *in glebas*, in the hard diffolution and eafie congelation, in their arifing in balls being burnt, and in
their precipitation : in fo much as it is probable, that
the bafis of Vitriol, is nothing but Allum. It is found
in minerall waters of two forts. The one, where the
very body and fubftance is diffolued : as in Cyprus,
which *Galen* defcribes, where the water is greene : alfo
at Smolnicium in Hungary, in Tranfiluania *ad Carpa-
tum montem*, at Nenfola, &c. In which places Copper is ordinarily made out of iron by infufing it in thefe
waters. I will not determine whether this be tranfmu-
tation of one fpecies into another, as fome doe hold, or
rather a precipitation of the Copper which was formerly diffolued in the water by meanes of the fharpe Vitriol ; which meeting with Iron, corrodes it, and imbi-
beth it, rather then the Copper, and fo lets the Copper
fall, and imbraceth the Iron in place of it. Wee daily
fee the like in Aqua fortis, which hauing imbibed one
metall, will readily embrace another that is more familiar to it, and let fall the firft. So Allum or Coppreffe
water hauing fome ftrong Lixiuium of tartar or other
calcind falt put to it, the Allum or Copprffe will
prefently fall to the bottome, and participate, and giue
place to the Lixiuium, as a thing more familiar to water, and of more eafie diffolution. But as I fay, I will
not determine this queftion, becaufe it is not much
pertinent to our bufineffe. Yet I will not omit the
iudgement of *Lazarus Ercker* the Emperours chiefe
Mine mafter in the Kingdome of Bohemia, who pro-
feffeth that he was long of this opinion, but altered it
vpon this reafon, That by exact proofe he found more

Copper

*Simp.med.facul.
l.9.c.61.*

*Libau.in Syntag.
3.part.l.7.
Item fingulariu
tart: 1.*

*Lib.3. Von.
Kupffer ertz.*

Copper ſtricken downe this way by Iron, then the water before did containe, and with the Copper ſome Siluer. The other kinde of Vitriol water is, where not the
body and ſubſtance of Vitriol is diſſolued, but the ſpirit, or vapour, or quality communicated to the water:
of this ſort are our Vitriol Baths for the moſt part. And
theſe are in themſelues wholſome, and are ſowre, if the
Vitriol be predominant. Such are moſt of our *Acidulæ*;
whereof we haue many in *Viterbio & Volaterano*, *Balneum ad morbum dictum*, Saurbrun by Franckford,
ad Oderam, &c. theſe are ſowre waters. Alſo from Allum, but milder, alſo from Sulphur, whoſe ſpririt or
vapour being burnt, is little differing from the ſpirit of
Vitriol, but ſomwhat ſalter. But the moſt part of our
Acidulæ are from Vitriol. This ſowre ſpirit of Allum,
Vitriol, or Sulphur, *Libavius* iudgeth with *Thomas
Iordanus* to be in the terreſtriall parts of theſe minerals,
becauſe it goes not away by boyling or diſtillation, and
therefore to be communicated with water by the corporall ſubſtance or iuyce of them. But that holds not
in minerall ſpirits which are heauier then water, as may
appeare by euaporation of any water made ſowre with
ſpirit of Vitriol or Sulphur, where, after long euaporation, that which remaines will be more ſowre then before euaporation. So it is alſo in Vinegar being a vegetable iuyce. The ſpirit of wine doth certainly ariſe firſt
in diſtillation, and the firſt is the beſt, being more volatill then the vapour of water. But this *ſpiritus acetoſus*
which is in Sulphur, Allum, Vitriol, and Vinegar, ariſeth laſt; and the more you diſtill away from, it the
ſharper it ariſeth, and the ſowrer is that which remayn-
eth. Thus much for Vitriol and concrete iuyces.

*Io. Baubinus de
thermis l. 2. c. 2.*

*De iudicio aqu.
miner. p. 2. c. 36.*

Cap. 8.

*Of minerall spirits. Quickſiluer, Sulphur or Brim-
ſtone, Arſenick, with his kindes ; Cadmia.*

A Fift kinde of mineralls are called ſpirits ; theſe are
volatill in the fire, and haue ingreſſion into metals,
but no metallin tuſion. Theſe are Quickſiluer, Sulphur,
Arſenick, Cadmia, Ruſma, &c. All which being volatill will eaſily ſublime, and being mixed with metals, as
Cadmia is ordinarily to make Braſſe, will alter the colour of the metall, and make it leſſe ſuſible, and leſſe
malleable. I will briefely run ouer the examples of theſe
and their virtues, or qualities, being more obſure and
in our Bathes leſſe vſefull then the former, and more
rare.

*Simpl. med; fa-
cult. l.9.c.59.*
Quickſiluer was not well knowne to *Galen*, for hee
confeſſeth that hee had no experience of it, and did
thinke it to be meerely artificiall, and not naturally bred
in the earth. *Dioſcorides* makes no mention of the temperature of it, but holds it to be a pernitious venome,
and to fret the entrayles : although *Mathiolus* affirmes
that it is ſafely giuen to women to further their deliue-
rance, and we find it ſo by often experience, both in that
cauſe, and in Wormes, and in the French Diſeaſe and
Leproſies, if it be skilfully prepared, and with iudgement
adminiſtred. *Fallopius* holds it to be one of the miracles
of nature. Thoſe that take vpon them to determine of
*Vidius Vidius
curat. generalim
p.2.ſect.2.l.3.
c.13.
Fallopius de
metallis c.37.*
the qualities of it, are much diſtracted; ſome reckoing it
to be hot and dry, and ſome cold and moiſt; and both in
a high degree. But in this account they conſider not
the qualities of the ingredients in the preparation; whether it be ſublim'd or precipitated. For my part I know
not how to reduce it to the Elementary qualities : nei-

ther am I afhamed of mine ignorance in it, feeing no
man hitherto hath giuen true fatisfaction herein. But
for our owne vfe where reafon failes vs, let vs be guided
by experience. We finde by experience, that it cuts,
attenuates, penetrates, melts, refolues, purges both *ad*
centrum & à centro, heats, cooles, &c, and is a tranfcen-
dent beyond our rules of Philofophie, and a monfter in
nature, as *Renodæus* faith. For our purpofe it is enough
to know whether it will impart any qualitie to water ;
which *Fallopius, Baccius, Solinander, Bauhinus,* and
Felix Platerus doe acknowledge. But it giues no tafte
to it, neither haue we many examples of Baths which
containe it. In Serra Morena in Spaine, neare the village Almedien is a Caue, where are many Wels, infected (as is thought) with Quickfiluer, becaufe much of
that minerall is extracted from thence, out of a red ftone
called *Minium natiuum.* About fifty miles from
thence in Valentiola there is another fountaine called
La Naua, of a fharpe tafte, and held to proceede from
Quickfiluer, and thefe waters are found wholfome. So
are the waters at Almagra and Toletum, and others by
the riuer Minius, which are hot. There are many venomous fprings attributed to Quickfiluer, as the red fountaine in Ethiopia, others in Boetia, Cæa in Trogloditis,
Stix in Archadia, Stix in Theffalia, Licus in Sicilia, &c:
which perhaps are from other mineralls, feeing wee
finde fome from Quickfiluer to be wholfome. For mines
of Quickfiluer, we read of many in Bætica, Attica, Ionia,
out of a ftone which *Pliny* cals *vomica liquoris æterni.*
In Germany at Landsberg, at Creucenachum, Schen-
bach, Beraun aboue Prage Kunningftien, &c. In Scotland, three miles beyond Barwicke, I found a red ftone,
which I take to be *minium natiuum,* feeing *Agricola*
makes mention of it in Scotland, but by a mifchance
could not try it.   Sul-

Sulpher attracts, contracts, resolues, mollifies, dis-
cusses, whereby it shewes a manifest heate, though not
intense, yet the fume of it is very soure, and therefore
must coole and dry : and I perswade my selfe that there
is no better fume to correct venomous and infectious
ayre, then this of Sulphur, or to remoue infections out
of roomes, clothes, bedding, vessels, &c. We must acknowledge parts in all compounded bodies ; as Rubarb
hath a purgatiue qualitie in the infusion, and an astri-
ctiue in the Terrestriall substance, where the salt hath
beene by infusion extracted. The substance of Sulphur
is very fat (*Sulphure nihil pinguius*) saith *Felix Platerus*) and this is the cause of his easie taking of fire, and
not any propinquitie it hath with fire in the qualitie of
heate : for if it were very hot, *Dioscorides* would not
commend it *purulenta extußientibus*, the next dore to a
Hectick. Also *Galen* saith, that fat things are moderately hot, and are rather nutriments then medicaments.
Now for Sulphurous Bathes, they are very frequent,
and if we should beleeue some, there are no hot Bathes,
but participate with Sulphur, but they are deceiued, as
shall appeare hereafter, when we come to shew the true
causes of the heate of Bathes. Neither are all sulphurous Bathes hot. *Gesner* reports of a Bath by Zurich, very cold, and yet sulphurous. *Agricola* of another by
Buda in Pannonia. In Campania by the Leucogæan
hils, are cold Springs full of Brimstone. Also there are
hot Bathes without any shew of sulphur that can be discerned, as the Bathes of Petriolum in Italy, the Bathes
Caldanellæ and *de Auinione in agro Senensi de Gratta
in Viterbiensi, de aquis in pisanis collibus, Divi Iohannis
in agro Lucensi in Alsatia*, another not farre from Ge-
bersallerum, &c. All which are very hot, and yet giue no
signe of Sulphur either by taste, or smell, or effects. And

yet

yet no doubt there are many Baths hauing a Sulphuri-
ous fmell from other minerals; as from Bitumen, Vitriol, Sandaracha, Allum, &c. which are hardly to be difcerned (if at all) from Sulphur. So we commonly fay,
if a houfe or a tree bee fet on fire by lightning, that it
fmels of Brimftone, when there was no Brimftone there.
Many things combufted will yeeld a Nitorous fmell,
not difcernable after burning, what the things were.
But there are diuers truly Sulphurous Baths which containe Sulphur, although not perfectly mixt with the
water without fome *medium*, but only confufed : for
perfect Sulphur will not diffolue in water, no more then
Bitumen. The fpirit of Sulpher may be communicated
to water, and fo may the matter of Sulphur before it
hath attained his perfect forme and confiftence : otherwife it is only confufed with water, and alters it into a
milky colour. *Sulphurea hac albus aqua.* At Baia are
diuers hot Sulphurous Baths, and euery where in He-
truria; in Sicily, *in Diocefi Panormitana*; the Baths of
Apono, as *Savanarola Muntagnana*, and *Fallopius* a-
uers, although *Iohn de Dondis* denieth it; the Bath of
Aftrunum, of Callatura, S. Euphemie, Aquifgran,
Brigenfis therma in Valefijs Helvetiorum, *aqua fancta
in Picenis*, and an infinite number euery where. *Baccius*
receiues our Baths of Bathe among Sulphurous Baths,
from the relation of *Edward Carne* when hee was Em-
baffadour to *Iulius tertius*, and *Paulus quartus*. I will
not deny fome touch of Sulphur in them, feeing wee
finde among Bitumeous coales, fome which are called
metall coales, with certaine yellow vaines which are
Sulphur. But the proportion of Sulphur to Bitumen, is
very little; and therefore I doe not hold them Sulphuri-
ous *à pradominio*. This is enough for Sulphur.

Concerning Arfenick, it is a venomous minerall, and

therefore

therefore I neede fpeake nothing of the Bathes which proceede from it, but that wee take heed of them; It is likely that thofe venomous waters and vapours which kill fuddenly, doe proceede from Arfenicke, as at Cicrum in Thracia *fons Neptunius in Terracina*, at Peraut by Mompelier, *the Lake Auernus. The caue of Charon by Naples.* Vnder Arfenicke wee may comprehend Auripigmentum, Rifagalum, Sandaracha, Rufma, &c. I heare of but one Mine of Rufma in Ciprus, from whence the Turkes haue it to take off hayre, and it doth it beft of any thing knowne, as *Bellonius* and *Platerus* reports, and I haue made triall of it oftentimes: The former forts of Arfenicke are found *in Miſſia Helleſponti in Ponto,* by the Riuer Hippanis, which is made bitter by it. In the leſſer Afia, betweene Magnefia and Euphefus in Carmania, &c. It is accounted to be extreame hot and putrefying.

Cadmia is either naturall or factitious: The naturall is often dangerous in Germany, as *Agricola* faith, efpecially that which is liquid, which is a ftrong corrofiue: the other is of the nature of Copper, moderately hot and clenfing, and efpecially good to cleere the eyes, as Calaminaris and Tutia. It is found in Copper Mynes, and of it felfe in Cyprus, as *Gallen* faith by the Citie Solos. Alfo in *Agro fenenfi, vicentino, Bergomenfi,* neere Como, where they make Braſſe with it. Vnder Mendip hils there is much of it. The Bathes of Saint *Caſſian* doe participate with it, and *Cicero* his Bathes neere Baia. Alfo the Bath at Zurich in Heluetia, and Grotta in Viterbio.

Thus much for Spirits.

C A P.

Cap. 9.

Of meane metals, or halfe metals: Bismutum or Tin-glaffe. Antimony. Bell-metall.

A Sixt fort I make to be meane metals, or halfe metals, which are minerall fubftances, hauing metalin fufion, but are not malleable as metals are: and therefore being mixt with metals, doe make them brittle. Thefe are *Bifmutum*, or *plumbum cinereum*, Anthimony, Bell-metall, which *Gaber* cals *Magnefia*, in dutch, *Speiff.* Calaem alfo may be reckoned among thofe, which is a kinde of white metalin Cadmia, brought out of the Eaft Indyes, which hath both metallin ingreffion, and metallin fufion, but not perfectly malleable. Thefe although they are more volatill then metall, yet by reafon of their fufion into a King, are not fo eafily fublimd as the Spirits.

Bifmutum is that wee call Tinglaffe, differing both from Tin and Leade. *Candidius nigro, fed plumbo nigrius albo.* It was not knowne to the Ancients, and therefore we can fay little of the qualities of it. It is found in England, and in Mifnia, and at Sneberg in Germany, and in very few places elfe. I reade not of any waters that participate with it : neither can I fay much of Antimony, but that *Diofcorides* faith it cooles, bindes, opens obftructions, &c. And *Gallen*, that it dryeth and bindeth, and is good for the eyes, &c. But of the purging qualitie they write nothing, although wee finde it to purge violently, both vpwards and downewards : whereupon wee may gather that all purging medicines are not hot, as I haue touched before. *Camden* faith there is a Mine of it in Cumberland: It is found in Italy, *in Thinni montibus, in Senenfi agro* in the Countie of
S. Flora,

S. Flora, and in Germany in many places. But J reade of no waters that participate with it, vnlesse wee should iudge all purgatiue waters to be infected with it:as neere Ormus, *Purchas* writes of such a Spring which purgeth.

Parte 3 pag. 72. *Sauonarola in Balneis Romandiolæ,* mentions a Spring at Meldula, which purgeth. Also *Balneum Tertutij in agro Pistoriensi, Fallopio;* also the sowre water of Mendich and Ponterbon doe purge choler, as *Rulandus* saith. At Nonesuch we haue also a purgatiue Spring, which may participate with Antimony or Niter, or both: But purgatiue waters are rare, vnlesse it be *ratione ponderis,* by the weight and quantity, and so any water may purge, and our Bath waters doe purge in that manner, and by the addition of Salt, which giues stimulation vnto it. This our Bath guides doe ordinarily prescribe to such as will be perswaded by them, not knowing how it agreeth with their griefes, nor how it may doe hurt in many respects, as oftentimes it doth.

Bell-metall is thought to be a mixture of Tinne and Copper Oares, as *Kentman* iudgeth, and is found in our Tinne and Copper Mynes in Cornewall. I reade of no waters infected with it, nor of any vse it hath in Physicke.

CAP. 10.

Of metals. Gold. Siluer. Iron. Copper. Tinne. Leade.

Fallop:de metallis cap. 10. *Libau,de nat. metall.part* 3. *cap.* 5.

THe seuenth and last sort are metals, minerall substances, fusible and malleable. These are commonly distinguished into perfect and imperfect; perfect, because they haue lesse impuritie or heterogeneitie in them, as gold & Siluer. The rest are called imperfect, because they

are full of impurities, and they are either hard or foft.
Hard, as thofe which will indure ignition before they
melt, as yron and Copper. Soft, which will not, but
melt at the firft, as Tinne and Lead.

Gold of all metals is the moft folid, and therefore the
moft heauie, as hauing no impurities or heterogeneall
fubftances mixed with it. And therefore it is not fub-
ieft to corruption, as other metals are, neither will it
loofe any of his fubftance, either by fire or water, al-
though it fhould be held in them a long time: fo as it is ^Baccius lib.6. cap. 8.^
an idle and vaine perfwafion that many haue, who
thinke by boyling Gold in broth, to get fome ftrength
from thence, and fo to make the brothes more cordiall. The like I may fay of putting Gold into Eleftuaries
or Pils, vnleffe it be in cafe of Quickfiluer taken into the
body, which the Gold by touch may gather to it, otherwife it goes out of the body as it came in, without any
concoftion or alteration, or diminution. And if it bee
diffolued in ftrong water, it will be reduced againe to his
metallin fubftance, without diminution, much leffe will
it be diffolued without corrofiue Spirits, to make *aurum
potabile*, as fome doe vndertake. *Crollius* doth acknow- ^Bafilica chimica pag.204.^
ledge, that there is but one *Menftruum* in the world
that may doe it, and that he knowes not. But if we had
it diffolued, we are yet vncertaine what the quality of it
would be, or what vfe to make of it in Phyficke; onely
becaufe it loofeth none of his fubftance, we know it can
doe no hurt, and therefore we vfe it for Cautoryes, and
to quench it in Beere or Wine, &c. to warme it, or to
giue it fome aftriftion from the fire. *Fallopius* in thefe ^De Thermis cap. 8.^
regards difclaymes it in all minerall waters, as hee doth
all other metals: and will not beleeue that any metall ^In ingreffu ad infirmos,^
doth impart any qualitie vnto water. *Claudius* holds o- ^pag. 373.^
therwife, and fo doth *Baccius, Sauonarola, Montagnana,*

Venuſtus Solinander, and almoſt all that haue written of
Bathes. For if we ſhould exclude Metals, wee muſt like.
wiſe exclude Stones, and Bitumina and Sulpher, and almoſt all minerals, except concrete iuyces. For none of
theſe, after they haue attayned to their full conſiſtence,
will of themſelues diſſolue in water, without the helpe
of ſome concrete iuyce, as a medium to vnite them with
the water. But before they haue their full conſiſtence,
whilſt they are in *Solutis principijs,* as Earth, Iuyce, or
Vapour, they may be communicated with water. Gold
is ſo ſparingly bred in the bowels of the earth, as in that
reſpect it can hardly furniſh a perpetuall Spring with a-
ny quality from it; yet ſome Bathes are held to participate with Gold, as *Ficuncellenſes, Fabariæ, Piperinæ, de
Grotta in Viterbio : Sancti Caſſiani de Buxo, &c.*

　　Siluer comes next in puritie to Gold, but is inferiour
vnto it, as appeares by the diſſolution of it, and by the
blew tincture which it yeelds, and by the fouling of the
fingers, &c. For the qualities of it, there is not much difcouered. But as all other things of pryce are ſuperſtiti-
ouſly accounted cordiall, ſo is this, eſpecially in hot and
moyſt diſtempers of the heart: for it is eſteemed to bee
cold, and dry, and aſtringent, and yet emollient. Wee
haue no Bathes which doe manifeſtly participate with
it : perhaps, by reaſon, nature doth not produce it in ſufficient quantitie to infect waters. *Iohn Bauhinus* thinkes
there may be Siluer in the Bathes at Boll : becauſe hee
ſaith there was a Pyritis or Marcheſit examined by Docter *Cadner,* and out of fiftie pound weight of it, hee
drew two drams of ſiluer: a very ſmall proportion to
ground his opinion vpon.

　　Iron is the moſt impure of all metals, as we haue it
wrought, and will hardly melt as metals ſhould doe, but
with additaments and fluſſes. Neither is it ſo malleable,

*Theod. Taber-
nimontanus. p.2.
cap 49.*

and duſtible as other metals are, by reaſon of his many
impurities. Yet we ſee that at Damaſco they worke and
refine it in ſuch ſort, at it will melt at a Lampe, and is ſo
tough, as it will hardly breake. And this is not by reaſon of any eſpeciall Myne differing from other iron
Mynes, for they haue no Mynes of yron neere to Da-
maſcus, as *Bellonius* reports, but haue it brought thither
from diuers other places, onely their art in working and
purifying it, is beyond ours. So the Spaniſh Steele and
iron is purer then ours, and wee doe eſteeme of Bilbo
blades beyond others which are quenched in the Riuer
Bilbilis: as *Turnus* his Sword in *Virgill* was quenched
in the Riuer Styx.

> *Enſem quem Dauno ignipotens Deus ipſe parenti*   Ænead. 12.
> *Fecerat, & Stygia candentem extinxerat unda.*

But the hardning of Steele lyeth not in this point; o-
ther waters no doubt may ſerue as well. But I perſwade
my ſelfe that our iron might be made much purer, and
perhaps ſome gold extraſted from it which it holds.

Concerning the temperature of Iron and Steele, *Ga-*   Simpl. lib. 9.
len reckons it among earth, and therefore it muſt bee
cold. *Manardus* is abſolutely of that opinion, and ſo   Lib. 16. Epiſt. 5.
are moſt of our Phyſitians. Only *Fallopius* holds it to   De metallis cap.
be hot, becauſe *Scribonius Largus* preſcribes it in vl-   20.
cers of the bladder, which it doth cure, not in regard   Simpl. lib. 4. c. 7.
of heating, but drying; for it dryeth and bindeth much,
and therefore by *Galens* rule it muſt bee cold. *Aſtrin-*
gentia omnia frigida. I haue obſerued in Iron and
Steele two diſtinſt qualities, The one opening, or deo-
pilatiue; the other aſtringent. The opening quality
lyeth in a volatill Salt or Niter, which it is full of, the
aſtringent qualitie in the Crocus, or Terreſtriall part.
Theſe two ſubſtances are thus diſcerned and ſeuered.
Take

Take of the fylings of Steele or Iron, and cast it into the flame of a candle, and you shall see it to burne like Salt-peter or Rosin. Take these fylings, and infuse them three or foure times in Water or Wine, as wee vse to make our Chalibert Wines, till the water or wine haue dissol-ued all this salt, and then dry it and cast it into the flame, and it shall not burne, but the liquor will haue a strong taste from this Salt. And this is it which opens obstructions. The astringent qualitie lyeth in the Ter-restriall substance, as is euident, after either, by infusions, or by calcination, the volutill salt is departed from it, that which remaines, is very astringent, and stayeth all manner of fluxes, &c.

Concerning Bathes participating with Iron, we haue too many examples of them for *Fallopius* to contra-dict. We may let him inioy his opinion of the *Calderi-ana, Veronensia & Villensia Lucensia,* although it bee a-gainst the iudgement of all other who haue written of them, and it is hard for him to be confident in a nega-tiue. Wee haue examples more then enough to proue the qualitie of Iron in our minerall waters. *Balneum Re-gina in agro Pisano,* is actually hot, and from iron. So is *Balneum Sancti Cassiani in agro Senensi :* So in *Bal-neum Ficuncella, de Russellis, Bora in agro. Florent. Brandula in agro Regiensi, Vesicatoriæ in Tuscia, Isenbrun* by Leige, *Forgense* in *Normandy:* the Spa water, Tun-bridge water; Bristoll water by S. *Vincents* Rocke : all which, some being hot and some cold participate with Iron, as may be proued, not onely by the consent of all writers, which haue made mention of them, but by the Mynes from whence they come, or by their taste, or by their vertues.

Copper comes neerest to the nature of Iron, but is more pure, and more easie of fusion, and will be almost
all

Solinander, pag. 193.
Venustus, pag. 159.
Baccius lib. 6. *cap.* 3
Sauonarola.
Renodæus pag: 306.

all conuerted into Vitrioll. They are conuertible the
one into the other, as I haue fhewed out of *Erker*, in Vi   *Libau. de nat.*
trioll. And by the practife at Commataw and Smolni-   *metall. c. 10.*
cium. The like alfo hath beene fhewed in Cornewall, at
the Confluence by Mafter *Ruffell*. *Ariftotle* alfo tels of a
Copper Myne in Thalia, an Iland of the Tyrrhen Sea,
which being wrought out, turned to an iron Myne : in
this fimilitude of nature, we cannot but iudge that there
is a fimilitude in qualities, and that Iron being cold,
Copper cannot be hot. Temperate it may be, becaufe
leffe aftringent then Iron, and more clenfing : *Rhafis*
faith that it purgeth like a Catharticum, and in his Con-
tinent, prefcribes it to purge water in dropfies. Another
argument that all purgatiues are not hot ; It drieth exceedingly, and attenuates and digefts. We haue diuers
waters which participate with it, which if they be pure
from Copper it felfe, are very fafe and wholefome : but
if they be foule, and proceede from the excrements of
Copper, they are not wholefome to drinke. *Balnea
Cellenfia feu ferina in Martiana Silua*, doe confift of
Copper and Allum. The Bath of Fabaria in Rhetia, of
Copper and Gold. *Aqua de Grotta in agro Viterbienfi*
is full of Copper; fo is *Aqua Iafielli*, *Balneum Leucen-
fe in Valefijs : Marcus Paulus Venetus*, tels of a greenifh
fountaine in Perfia, which purgeth exceedingly, and is
held to come from Copper.

Tinne and Lead are two of our Staple commodities
which our Countrie yeelds plentifully, not onely for our
owne vfe, but to fupply other Nations. Tinne is bred in
Cornwall, and part of Deuonfhire, and in the Ifles of
Silly, which from thence were called *Caffiterides*. It is
melted out of little blacke ftones, which the Dutch call
Zwitter, with great charge, becaufe they cannot melt it,
but with wood coales, which is brought them farre off,

H   and

and they are faine to runne it ouer two or three times, before they can get out all the Tinne, and yet much of it is wasted in the blast. I doubt not but it might bee done with Sea-Coale, if they knew the Artifice, and with a great product of Tinne. There is both siluer and gold found in it, but without wasting of the Tinne, wee know no meanes to seuer it. It is in qualitie cold and dry, and yet moues sweat abundantly, as I haue proued.

Lead is melted commonly out of an Oare common to Siluer and Lead, as *Pliny* saith, called *Galena*. And although *Agricola* saith of the villachar Lead, that it holds no Siluer, and therefore fittest for assayes; yet *Lazarus Ercker* contradicts it out of his owne experience. Our Countrie abounds with it euery where, especially at the Peake in Darbishire, and at Mendip in Sommersetshire; Wales also and Cornwall, and Deuon, are full of it, and so is Yorkeshire and Cumberland. The qualities of it are cold and dry. But for these two metals, wee finde no waters which are infected with them. In Lorayne, they haue Bathes called *Plumbaria*, which some thinke by reason of the name, to proceede from Lead: but *Iohn Bauhinus* thinkes they should bee called *plumiers*, as *Pictorius* writes it from the French word *plumer, a deplumando*, because they are so hot, as they vse to scald fowles in them, to take off their feathers.

Pag. 90.

Thus much for metals, and all other sorts of Minerals, with their seuerall Natures and Bathes infected with any of them. As for mixed Bodies, and flores, and recrements, &c. they are to be referred to the simple bodies from whence they proceede: As *Tutia, Pompholix: Minium, Cerussa, Sublimatum, Præcipitatum, &c.*

CAP.

CAP. II.

Of the generation of metals in the earth. Their femi-
nary spirit, matter.

NOw I muſt ſhew the generation of theſe minerals
in the bowels of the earth, which of neceſſity wee
muſt vnderſtand, before wee can ſhew the reaſons how
minerall waters receiue either their actuall heat, or their *Fallop.de me-*
vertues. *tallis cap.11.*
Libauius de nat.
Some haue imagined that metals and minerals were *metal.cap.12.*
created perfect at the firſt, ſeeing there appeares not any
ſeede of them manifeſtly, as doth of Animals and Vegetables; and ſeeing their ſubſtances are not ſo fluxible, but
more firme and permanent. But as they are ſubiect to
corruption in time, by reaſon of many impurities, and
differing parts in them, ſo they had need to be repaired
by generation.

It appeares in *Geneſis*, that Plants were not created
perfect at firſt, but onely in their Seminaries: for *Moſes*,
Cap. 2. giues a reaſon why Plants were not come forth
of the earth, ſcil. becauſe (as *Tremellius* tranſlates it)
there had as yet neither any raine fallen, nor any dew
aſcended from the earth, whereby they might be produced and nouriſhed : The like we may iudge of minerals, that they were not at firſt created perfect, but diſpoſed of in ſuch ſort, as they ſhould perpetuate themſelues in their ſeuerall kindes. Wherefore it hath euer
beene a receiued *Axiome*, among the beſt Philoſophers,
that minerals are generated, and experience hath confirmed it in all kindes. Our Salt peter men finde that
when they haue extracted Salt peter out of a floore of
earth one yeare, within three or foure yeares after, they
finde more Salt-peter generated there, and doe worke it
ouer

ouer againe. The like is obſerued in Allum and Cope-
roſſe.

And for metals, our Tinners in Cornewall haue experience of Pitts which haue beene filled vp with earth
after they haue wroughtout all the Tinne they could
finde in them; and within thirty yeares they haue ope-
ned them againe, and found more Tinne generated.
The like hath beene obſerued in Iron, as *Gaudentius Me-*
rula reports of *Ilua*, an Iland in the Adriaticke Sea, vnder the Venetians, where the Iron breedes continually
as faſt as they can worke it, which is confirmed alſo by
Agricola and *Baccius*: and by *Virgill* who ſaith of it, *Il-*
lua inexhauſtis Chalybum generoſa metallis. The like we
reade of at Saga *in Lygÿs*, where they dig ouer their
Iron Mynes euery tenth yeare. *Iohn Matheſius* giues vs
examples, almoſt of all ſorts of minerals and metals,
which he hath obſerued to grow and regenerate. The
like examples you may finde in *Leonardus Thurneiſe-*
rus. *Eraſtus* affirmes that hee did ſee in S. *Ioachims*
dale, ſiluer growne vpon a beame of wood, which was
placed in the pit to ſupport the workes: and when it
was rotten, the workemen comming to ſet new timber
in the place, found the ſiluer ſticking to the old beame.
Alſo he reports that in Germany, there hath beene vnripe and vnconcocted ſiluer found in Mynes, which the
beſt workemen affirmed, would become perfect ſiluer in
thirty yeares. The like *Modeſtinus Fachius*, and *Mathe-*
ſius affirme of vnripe and liquid ſiluer; which when the
workemen finde, they vſe to ſay *Wee are come too ſoone.*
But I neede not produce any more proofes for this purpoſe, as I could out of *Agricola* and *Libauius*, and others,
ſeeing our beſt Philoſophers, both ancient and moderne, doe acknowledge that all minerals are generated.
The manner of generation of minerals and metals, is the

ſame

Lib. 3. c. 19.

In Sarept. conci.
3. 11. &c.

In Alchimia
magna.
De metallis pag.
17. & 19.

Sebaſt. Foxius
l. 3. c. 6.
Seuerinus c. 8.
p. 125.

same in all, as is agreed vpon both by *Plato* and *Aristotle*, and *Theophrastus* : the difference is in the efficient, and in the matter.

For the manner of generation of minerals, although it be alike in all, yet it differs from the generation of animate bodies, whether animals or vegetables, in this, that hauing no seede, they haue no power or instinct of producing other indiuiduals, but haue their species perpetuated *per virtutem seu spiritum semini analogum*, by a spirituall substance proportionable to seede, which is not resident in euery indiuiduall, as it is in animals and Plants, but in their proper wombes. This is the iudgement of *Petrus Seuerinus*, howsoeuer hee doth obscure it by his Platonicall grandiloquence. And as there is not *Vacuum in Corporibus*, so much lesse in *Speciebus*. For that the Species are perpetuated by new generations, is most certaine, and proued before : that it is not out of the seedes of indiuiduals, is euident by this, that if minerals doe not assimulate nourishment by attraction, retention, concoction, expulsion, &c. for the maintenance of their owne indiuiduall bodies, much lesse are they able to breede a superfluitie of nourishment for seede. And how can they attract and concoct nourishment, and expell excrements, which haue no vaines nor fibres, nor any distinct parts to performe these Offices withall ? Moreouer they are not increased as Plants are, by nourishment, whereas the parts already generated, are extended in all proportions by the ingression of nutriment, which fils and enlarges them: but onely are augmented externally vpon the superficies, by superaddition of new matter concocted by the same vertue and spirit, into the same Species.

The matter whereof Mineralls are bred, is much controuerted, *Aristotle* makes the humidity of water and the

Cesalpinus de metal.l.1.c.2.

Cap. 2.

Erast. disput. part.2.p.262

the dryneſſe of earth to bee the matter of all Mineralls : the dryneſſe of earth to participate with fire, and
the humidity of water with ayre, as *Zabarella* interprets it ; ſo that to make a perfect mixt body, the foure
Elements doe concurre : and to make the mixture more
perfect, theſe muſt be reſolued into vapour or exhalation by the heat of fire, or influence from the Sunne and
other Planets, as the efficient cauſe of their generation :
but the cauſe of their congelation to bee cold in ſuch
bodies as heat will reſolue. This vapour conſiſting
partly of moyſture, and partly of dryneſſe, if all the
moyſture be ſpent, turnes to earth or ſalt, or concrete
iuyces, which diſſolue in moyſture : if ſome moyſture
remaine before congelation, then it turnes to ſtone : if
this dry exhalation be vnctuous, and fat, and combu-
ſtible, then Bitumen, and Sulphur, and Orpiment are
bred of it : if it be dry and incombuſtible, then concrete
iuyces, &c. But if moyſture doe abound in this vapour,
then metals are generated which are fuſible and malleable. And for the perfecting of theſe generations, this
exhalation is not ſufficient, but to giue them their due
conſiſtence, there muſt be the helpe of cold from Rocks
in the earth to congeale this exhalation. So that here
muſt be two efficients, heat and cold. And for the better effecting of this , theſe exhalations doe inſinuate
themſelues into ſtones, in the forme of dew or froſt,
that is, in little graines ; but differing from dew and
froſt in this, that theſe are generated after that the vapour is conuerted to water ; whereas Minerals are
generated before this conuerſion into water. But there
is doubt to be made of froſt, becauſe that is bred before
the conuerſion of the exhalation into water, as may appeare, *Meteor.* 1. According to this aſſertion there muſt
be two places for the generation of minerals : the one a

Eraſtus, Careri-
us, Ceſalpinus,
Martinus,
Moreſinus,
Foxius, Magy-
rus, Libavius.

3 *Meteor. c.ult.*
Ceſalp. l.3.c.1.

Libau.de nat.
metall c.14.
Carerius 178.

Septal. in Hipp.
de aere, aqu. &c.

matrix, where they receiue their essence by heat in forme of an exhalation, and from thence they are sent to a second place to receiue their congelation by the coldnesse of Rocks : and from this *matrix* come our minerall waters, aud not from the place of congelation.

This is the generation of minerals, according to *Aristotle* ; but it is not so cleare, but that it leaues many scruples, both concerning the matter, and the efficients. For the matter, it seemes not probable, that water and earth should make any thing but mudde and dirt ; for you can expect no more from any thing then is in it, the one is cold and dry, the other cold and moyst ; and therefore as fit to be the matter of any other thing, as of particular mineralls. And water, whereof principally metals are made to consist, is very vnfit to make a malleable and extentible substance, especially being congeled by cold, as we may see in yce. But some doe adde a minerall quality to these materials, and that simple water is not the chiefe matter of metals, but such as hath imbibed some minerall quality, and so is altered from the nature of pure water. This assertion doth presuppose mineralls in the earth before they were bred : otherwise what should breed them at the first, when there was no minerall quality to be imparted to water ? Againe, this minerall quality either giues the water or the vapour of it the essence of the minerall, and then it is not the effect of water, but of the minerall quality, or the potentiall faculty to breed it. If the essence, then this metallin water, or vapour, must haue the forme of the metall, and so be fusible and malleable. If it haue only the power and potentiall faculty, then the generation is not perfected, but must expect further concoction. This concoction is said to be partly by heat, and partly
by

by cold ; if by heat, it muſt be in the paſſages of the exhalation as it is carried in the bowels of the earth : for, afterwards when the exhalation is ſetled in the ſtones, the heat is gone. Now if the concoction bee perfected before the exhalation be inſinuated into the Stones, as it muſt be, if it be like dew, then is it perfect metall, and neither is able to penetrate the Stones, nor hath any neede of the cold of them to perfect the generation. If by cold, it is ſtrange that cold ſhould be made the principall agent in the generation of metals, which generates nothing; neither can heate be the efficient of theſe generations. Simple qualities can haue but ſimple effects, as heate can but make hot, cold can but coole, &c. But they ſay cold doth congeale metals, becauſe heate doth diſſolue them; I anſwer, that the rule is true, if it bee rightly applied: as wee ſee yce which is congealed by cold, is readily diſſolued by heate. But the fuſion of metals cannot properly bee called a diſſolution by heate, becauſe it is neither reduced to water or vapour, as it was before the congelation by cold, nor is it permanent in that kinde of diſſolution, although after fuſion it ſhould be kept in a greater heat then cold could be which congealed it. For the cold in the bowels of the earth cannot be ſo great, as it is vpon the ſuperficies of the earth, ſeeing it was neuer obſerued that there was any yce bred there. Wherefore this diſſolution which is by fuſion, tends not to the deſtruction of the metal (but doth rather make it more perfect) as it ſhould doe according to the former rule rightly applied. And therefore this diſſolution by fuſion, doth not argue a congelation by cold: which being in the paſſiue elements, doth rather attend the matter then the efficient of generations: for it is apt to dull and hebetat all faculties and motions in nature, and ſo to hinder generations, rather then to

Valeſius ſacra philoſoph. c. 49.

further

further any. It is heate and moyſture that further generations, as *Ouid* ſaith, *Quippe vbi temperiem ſumpſere
humorque calorque, Concipiunt.*

And thus much for *Ariſtotles* generation of minerals, where his vapours or exhalations doe rather ſerue
for the collection or congregation of matter in the
Mynes, then for the generation of them; as *Libauius* *Singularium*
doth rightly iudge. *Agricola* makes the matter of mine- *lib. 1. part. 1*
rals to be *Succus Lapideſcens Metallificus, &c.* and with
more reaſon, becauſe they are found liquid in the earth :
Gilgill would haue it Aſhes; *Democritus* Lyme : but
theſe two being artificiall matters, are no where found
in the earth. The Alchymiſts make Sulphur and
Mercurie the matter of metals : *Libauius,* Sulphur *De nat. metal.*
and Vitrioll. But I will not ſtand vpon diſcourſing of *cap. 10.*
theſe materials, becauſe it makes little to my purpoſe. It
is enough for my purpoſe to ſhew the manner of theſe
generations, which I take to be this.

There is a Seminarie Spirit of all minerals in the
bowels of the earth, which meeting with conuenient
matter and adiuuant cauſes, is not idle, but doth proceed
to produce minerals, according to the nature of it, and
the matter which it meetes withall : which matter it
workes vpon like a ferment, and by his motion procures
an actuall heate, as an inſtrument to further his worke;
which actuall heate is increaſed by the fermentation of
the matter. The like we ſee in making of malt, where
the graynes of Barley being moyſtened with water, the
generatiue Spirit in them, is dilated, and put in action;
and the ſuperfluitie of water, being remoued, which
might choake it, and the Barley laid vp in heapes; the
Seedes gather heat, which is increaſed by the contiguitie of many graines lying one vpon another. In this
worke natures intent is to produce moe indiuiduals,

I

according to the nature of the Seede, and therefore it
shootes forth in spyres: but the Artist abuses the intention of nature, and conuerts it to his end, that is, to in-
creafe the fpirits of his Malt. The like we finde in minerall fubftances, where this fpirit or ferment is refident,
as in Allum and Copperos mynes, which being broken,
expofed and moyftened, will gather an actuall heate,
and produce much more of thofe minerals, then elfe the
myne would yeeld: As *Agricola* and *Thurneifer* doe
affirme, and is proued by common experience. The like
is generally obferued in Mynes, as *Agricola, Eraftus,
Libauius, &c.* doe auouch out of the daily experience
of minerall men, who affirme, that in moft places, they
finde their Mynes fo hot, as they can hardly touch
them: although it is likely that where they worke for
perfect minerals, the heate which was in fermentation,
whilft they were yet breeding, is now much abated: the
minerals being now growne to their perfection. And
for this heate wee neede not call for the helpe of the
Sunne, which a little cloude will take away from vs,
much more the body of the earth, and Rocks; nor for
fubterraneall fire: this imbred heate is fufficient, as may
appeare alfo by the Mynes of Tinglaffe, which being
digged, and laid in the moyft ayre, will become very
hot. So Antimony and Sublimat being mixed together,
will grow fo hot as they are not to be touched: If this be
fo in little quantities, it is likely to bee much more in
great quantities and huge rockes. Heate of it felfe dif-
Carerius p 213. fers not in kinde, but onely in degree, and therefore is
inclined no more to one Species, then to another, but as
it doth attend and ferue a more worthy and fuperiour
faculty, fuch as this generatiue fpirit is. And this fpirit
doth conuert any apt matter it meetes withall to his
owne Species, by the helpe of heate; and the earth is

full of such matter which attends vpon the Species of things : and oftentimes for want of fit opportunitie and adiuuant causes, lyes idle, without producing any Species: but is apt to be tranfmuted by any mechanicall and generatiue ſpirit into them. And this matter is not the Elements themſelues, but ſubterraneall Seeds placed in the Elements, which not being able to liue to themſelues, doe liue vnto others. This ſeminarie Spirit is acknowledged by moſt of *Ariſtotles* interpreters, (and *Moriſinus* cals it *Elpheſteria*) not knowing how otherwiſe to attribute theſe generations to the Elements. And this is the cauſe why ſome places yeeld ſome one minerall ſpecies aboue another. *Quippe ſolo natura ſubeſt. Non omnis fert omnia tellus.* The ſeminary Spirit hath his proper wombs where it reſides, and formes his Species according to his Nature, and to the aptneſſe of his matter. But as *Seuerinus* affirmes of animall ſeedes, that they are in themſelues *Hermaphroditicall*, and neither maſculine nor feminine, but as they meete with ſuperuenient cauſes, ſo it is in theſe minerall Seedes and Species, which in one wombe doe beget diuers ſorts of minerals, either according to the aptneſſe of the matter, or the vigour of the Spirits. Thus much for the generation of minerals, &c.

Foxius , Martinus, Moreſinus, Magyrus, Libauius, Velcurio, Valeſius, Carerius, Eraſtus, Severinus.

Cap. 10.

Of the cauſes of actuall heat, and medicinable virtue in minerall waters. Diuers opinions of others, reiected.

NOw I come to ſhew how our minerall waters receiue both their actuall heat, and their virtues. I

ioyne them together, becaufe they depend vpon one
and the fame caufe, vnleffe they bee iuyces which will
readily diffolue in water, without the helpe of heat : o-
ther minerals will not, or very hardly.

This actuall heat of waters haue troubled all thofe
that haue written of them, and many opinions haue
beene held of the caufes of them.

Some attribute it to wind, or ayre, or exhalations
included in the bowels of the earth, which either
by their owne nature, or by their violent motion,
and agitation, and attrition vpon rocks and narrow
paffages, doe gather heat, and impart it to our waters.
Of their owne nature thefe exhalations cannot bee fo
hot, as to make our water hot, efpecially feeing in
their paffage among cold rocks, it would bee much al-
laied, hauing no fupply of heat to maintaine it. Moreouer, where water hath paffage to get forth to the fuperficies of the earth, there thefe exhalations and winds
will eafily paffe, and fo their heat gone withall, and fo
our waters left to their naturall coldneffe : whereas wee
fee they doe continue in the fame degree and tenor, many generations together. If by their agitation and violent motion they get this heat, becaufe no violent thing
is perpetuall or conftant: this cannot be the caufe of the
perpetuall and conftant heat of water. Befides, this
would rather caufe earthquakes and ftormes, and noy-
fes in the earth, then heat our fprings. Moreouer, wee
dayly obferue that water is neuer heated by winds, or
agitation ; as in the Cataracts of the Rhein by Splug;
the agitation and fall of water vpon rocks is moft violent, and makes a hydeous noyfe ; yet it heats not
the water, though it be very deepe in the earth. Neither can any attrition heat either ayre, or water, or any
foft, and liquid thing, but rather make it more cold.

Valefius contro.
lib.4.cap.3.
Solinand.l.1.c.4.

Others

Others attribute this actuall heat of Baths vnto the Sunne, whose beames peircing through the pores of the earth, doe heat our waters. The Sunne by his light and beames, no doubt, doth warme these inferiour parts, especially where they haue free passage, and reflection withall, and it is to be iudged, that the heat not being essentially in the Sunne, is an effect of the light by whose beames it is imparted to vs. So as where light is excluded, heat is also excluded. And if wee can exclude the heat of the Sunne by the interposition of a mud wall, or by making a Cellar six foot vnder the ground; how is it likely that these beames can peirce so deepe into the earth, as to heat the water there? as *Lucretius* saith.

Qui queat hic subter tam crasso corpore terram   *Lib.6.*
Percoquere humorem, & calido sociare vapori?
Prasertim cum vix possit per septa domorum
Insinuare suum radijs ardentibus astum.

And if the Sunne be not able to heat a standing Poole in the middest of Summer, how should it heat a subterraneall water, which is alwayes in motion, especially in the winter time? Againe, if this heat come from the Sunne, then in the Summer, when the Sun is hottest, the waters should be so also, and in winter cold, because of the absence of the Sunne; but we finde them alwayes alike. Neither can any Antiperistasis be equiualent to the Sunnes presence to continue their heat. It should rather diminish it by the opposite quality of cold: for, adde cold to any heat, and the cold by working vpon the heat, doth bring it to a temper, and makes the heat lesse; otherwise how should a temperament arise from *Vales. cont.c.5.* the mixture of the Elements, if there were not a reacti- *Magyrusl.3.c.3* on, and a refiftence, which reduceth the mixture to his temperament. Wherefore this Antiperiftafis is an idle inuention to maintaine this purpofe.

Others attribute this actuall heat to quick Lyme, which we fee doth readily heat any water caft vpon it, and alfo kindle any combuftible fubftance put into it; this is *Democritus* his opinion. To this I anfwer, that Lyme is an artificiall thing, not naturall, and is neuer found in the bowels of the earth. Befides, if it were found, one infufion of water extinguifheth the heat of it, and then it lyeth like a dead earth, and will yeeld no more heat. So as this cannot procure a perpetuall heat to Baths : neither can the Lymeftones without calcination, yeeld any heat to water, nor will breake and crackle vpon the affufion of water, as Lyme doth. Wherefore this opinion is altogether improbable.

Others attribute this actuall heat to a fubterraneall fire kindled in the bowels of the earth vpon Sulphur and Bitumen. Now we are come to hell, which *Pitha-*
Metamorph.15. *goras* cals *Materiam Vatum, falfique pericula mundi*; The dreame of Poets, and a forged feare. The largeft defcription of it is in *Virgill* : from whence both Diuines and Philofophers deriue much matter : and *Baccius* doth beleeue that there is fuch a thing in the center of the earth. But if we obferue *Virgill* well, we fhall finde that he propounds it but as a dreame : for in the end of that booke he faith

Ænead.6.
Sunt geminæ fomni portæ; quarum altera fertur
Cornea, qua veris facilis datur exitus umbris :
Altera candenti perfecta nitens Elephanto,
Sed falfa ad Cœlum mittunt infomnia manes.

Dreames haue two gates, the one is said to be
Of Horne, through which all true conceits do flee:
The other framed all of Iuory rare,
But lets out none, but such as forged are.

Now saith he, when *Anchyses* had led *Æneas* and
Sibilla through Hell, hee lets them forth at the Iuory
gate (*Portaque emittit Eburna:*) As if he should say;
all that I haue related of hell, is but a fiction; and thus
Ludouicus Viues interprets it, in his comment vpon this
place.

I hope none will thinke that I deny a Hell, but I ap-
proue not of the assignement of it to the center of the
earth, or that that fire should serue, as *Baccius* would haue
it, to further all generations in the earth: and as others,
to be the cause of Fountaines, Windes, Earth-quakes,
Vulcanoes Stormes, Saltnesse of the Sea, &c. nor of the
actuall heate of our Bathes, although it be the most common receiued opinion.

First for the place, it is not likely that the center of
the earth, whither all heauie things doe tend, should be
hollow, but rather more compact then any other part
of the earth, as likewise *Valesius* thinkes: but if there bee
any concauities, they are betweene the Center and the
Superficies; and these concauities being receptacles of
water from the Sea, cannot also receiue fire. These two
will not agree together in one place, but the one will
expell the other : for whereas some hold that Bitumen
will burne in water, and is nourished by it, it is absolute-
ly false, as experience shewes; and I haue touched it a-
mong the Bitumina.

Moreouer, if the heate which warmes our Bathes did
proceede from hence, there must be huge vessels aboue
the fire to containe water, whereby the fire might heate

Agricola.
Baccius lib. 1,
cap. 19.

it, and not be quenched by it. Also the vapours arising
from hence, must bee hotter then water can endure, or
be capable of: for as they ascend towards the Superficies of the earth, they must needes bee cooled as they
passe by rockes, or else they could not be congealed into water againe: and after this congelation, the water
hath lost most of his heate, as we finde in our ordinary
distillations of Rose water, &c. where we see our water
to descend into the receiuer, almost cold; so that they
cannot deriue our hot Bathes from hence.

Secondly, for the fire it selfe, although water and ayre
may be receiued into the bowels of the earth, yet there
is great difficulty for fire. For the other two neede no
nourishment to support them, as fire doth. If there bee
not competencie of ayre to nourish the fire, howsoeuer
there be fewell enough, it is suddenly quenched, and such
huge fire as this must be, will require more ayre, then
can there be yeelded: a great part thereof passing away
through the secret creekes of rocks, and little or none
entring through the Sea. And therefore daily experience shewes, that our minerall men are faine to sinke new
Shafts (as they call them) to admit ayre to their works,
otherwise their lights would goe out. Although one
would thinke that where many men may haue roome
enough to worke, there would be space enough for ayre
to maintaine a few lights. The like we see in Cupping-
glasses, where the light goes out as soone as they are applied. Also there are no fires perpetuall, as hot Bathes
are, but are either extinct, or keepe not the same tenor.
Wherefore fire cannot bee the cause of this constant
heate of Bathes. Also where fire is, there will be smoake,
for as it breedes exhalations, so it sends them forth. But
in most of our hot Bathes wee finde none of these dry
exhalations. Moreouer fire is more hardly pend in then
ayre:

ayre, yet we fee that ayre doth breake forth: wherefore fire fhould alfo make his way, hauing fewell enough to maintaine it. So they fay it doth in our Vulcanoes at Hecla in Ifeland, Ætna in Sicily: Vefuuio in Campania: in Enaria, Æolia, Lipara,&c. But it is yet vnproued that thefe eruptions of fire, doe proceede from any deepe caufe, but onely are kindled vpon or neere the fuperficies of the earth, where there is ayre enough to feede it, and meanes enough to kindle it by lightnings, or other cafuall meanes. Whereas in the bowels of the earth, there is neither ayre to nourifh it, nor any meanes to kindle it: feeing neither the beames of the Sunne, nor Winde, or other exhalations, nor Lyme, nor Lightnings, can doe it. For the fame reafons that exclude the beames of the Sunne and exhalations, will likewife exclude Lightnings.

Thirdly, for the fewell, there are onely two fubftances in the bowels of the earth, which are apt fewels for fire, Bitumen and Sulpher.

Sulpher is in fuch requeft with all men, as they think *Donatius de aquis lucenfibus lib.1.cap.8.* there can be no hot Bath without it: nay many hold, that if water doe but paffe through a myne of Brimftone, although it be not kindled, but actually cold, yet it will contract from thence, not onely a potentiall, but an actuall heate. But we doe manifeftly finde, that neither all hot waters are fulphurous, nor all fulphurous waters hot (as is faid before in Sulpher.)

The Bathes of Caldanella and Auinian, *in agro Senenfi, De Grotta in viterbio, De aquis in pifano, Diui Iohannis in agro Lucenfi, Balneum Geberfuilleri in Halfatia,* &c. are all hot, and yet giue no figne of fulphur, either by fmell or tafte, or qualitie, or effect. Contrariwife that all fulphurous waters are not hot, may appeare by the Bathes of Zurich in Heluetia, of Buda in Pannonia, at

K   Cure

Cure in Rhetia, Celenſes in Germany. In Campania, betweene Naples and Buteolum, are many cold ſulphurous Springs. At *Brandula in agro Carpenſi, &c.* All which Bathes ſhew much Sulphur to be in them, and yet are cold. And no meruaile, for if we infuſe any ſimple, be it neuer ſo hot potentially, yet it will not make the liquor actually hot. Wherefore this Sulphur muſt burne before it can giue any actuall heate to our Bathes; and then it muſt needes be ſubiect to the former difficulties, and alſo muſt bee continually repaired by new generations of matter, which actuall fire cannot further, but rather hinder. The fire generates nothing, but conſumes all things.

The like we may iudge of Bitumen, that vnleſſe it be kindled, it can yeeld no heate to our Bathes: as *Solinander* reports of a Bituminous Myne in VVeſtfalia *in agro Tremonenſi*, where going downe into the groue, hee found much water, hauing the ſmell, taſte, and colour of Bitumen, and yet cold. *Agricola* imputes the chiefe cauſe of the heating of Bathes, vnto the ſewell of Bitumen, *Baccius* on the other ſide to Sulphur. But in mine opinion, they need not contend about it. For as I haue ſhewed before in the examples of minerall waters, there are many hot Springs, from other minerals, where neither Sulphur nor Bitumen haue beene obſerued to be. *Iohn de Dondis,* and *Iulius Alexandrinus*, were much vnſatisfied in theſe opinions, and did rather acknowledge their ignorance, then that they would ſubſcribe vnto them. I neede not diſpute whether this fire be *in Alueis,* or *in Canalibus,* or *in Vicinis partibus, &c.* be cauſe I thinke it is in neither of them.

Lib.1.c ult.

C A P.

Cap. 13.

The Authors opinion concerning the cause of actuall heat, and medicinable virtue in minerall waters.

WHerefore finding all the former opinions to bee doubtfull and weakely grounded, concerning the causes of the actuall heat of Baths : let me presume to propound another, which I perswade my selfe to bee more true and certaine. But because it hath not beene mentioned by any Author that I know, I haue no mans steps to follow in it.

Avia Doctorum peragro loca, nullius ante Trita solo.

I trauell where no path is to be seene
Of any learned foot that here hath beene.

Which makes me fearfull in the deliuery of it. But if I doe erre in it, I hope I shall not be blamed ; seeing I doe it in disquisition of the truth.

I haue in the former Chapter set downe mine opinion concerning the generation of minerals ; that they haue their seminaries in the earth replenished with spirits, and faculties attending them : which meeting with conuenient matter and adiuuant causes, doe proceede to the generation of seuerall species, according to the nature of the efficient and aptnesse of the matter. In this worke of generation, as there is *generatio unius,* so there must be *corruptio alterius.* And this cannot bee done without a superiour power, which by moysture, dilating it selfe, worketh vpon the matter, like a ferment to bring it to his owne purpose. This motion betweene

the agent fpirit, and the patient matter, produceth an
actuall heat *(ex motu fit calor)* which ferues as an inftrument to further this worke. For as cold duls, and be-
numbes all faculties, fo heat doth quicken them. This
I fhewed in the example of Malt. It is likewife true in
euery particular grayne of Corne, fowen in the ground,
although by reafon they lye fingle, their actuall heat is
not difcernable by touch ; yet wee finde that externall
heat and moyfture doe further their fpiring, as adiuuant
caufes : where the chiefe agent is the generatiue fpirit
in the feed. So I take it to bee in minerals, with thofe
diftinctions before mentioned. And in this all generations agree, that an actuall heat, together with moyfture, is requifite : otherwife there can neither be the
corruption of the one, nor the generation of the other.
This actuall heat is leffe fenfible in fmall feeds and tender bodyes, then it is in the great and plentifull generations, and in hard and compact matter : for hard
bodies are not fo eafily reduced to a new forme, as tender bodies are ; but require both more fpirit, and longer time to be wrought vpon. And therefore whereas
vegetable generations are brought to perfection in a few
moneths, thefe minerall generations doe require many
yeares, as hath beene obferued by minerall men. Moreouer, thefe generations are not terminated with one
production, but as the feed gathereth ftrength by enlarging it felfe ; fo it continually proceeds to fubdue
more matter vnder his gouernment : fo as, where once a-
ny generation is begun, it continues many ages, and feldome giues ouer. As we fee in the Iron mynes of Ilma,
the Tinne mynes in Cornwall, the Lead mynes at
Mendip, and the Peake, &c. which doe not only ftretch
further in extent of ground, then haue beene obferued
heretofore ; but alfo are renewed in the fame groues
                                                        which

which haue beene formerly wrought, as our Tinners in
Cornewall doe acknowledge; and the examples of *Ilma* Cap.111
and *Saga* before mentioned doe confirme. This is a suf-
ficient meanes for the perpetuitie of our hot Springs :
that if the actuall heate proceede from hence, there
neede be no doubt of the continuance of them, nor of
their equall Tenor or degree of heate.

Now for the nature of this heate, it is not a destructiue
heate, as that of fire is, but a generatiue heate ioyned
with moysture. It needes no ayre for euentilation, as
the other doth. It is in degree hot enough for the hottest Bathes that are, if it bee not too remote from the
place where the water issueth forth. It is a meanes to impart the qualities of minerals to our waters, as well as
heate, by reason the minerals are then *in solutis principijs,*
in their liquid formes, and not consolidated into hard
bodies. For when they are consolidated, there are few of
them that will yeeld any quality to water, vnlesse they
be the concrete iuyces, or any actuall heate, because that
is procured by the contiguity of bodies, when one part
lyeth vpon another, and not when they are growne *In
corpus continuum.* As we see in Malt, where by turning
and changing the contiguitie, the heate is increased, but
by suffering it to vnite, is quenched : But before consolidation, any of them may yeeld either Spirit, or Iuyce,
or Tincture to the waters, which by reason of their tenuitie (as is said before) are apt to imbybe them. Now if
actuall fire kindled in the earth, should meete with these
minerals, whilst they are in generation, it would dissi- *Thurneiser Al-*
pate the Spirits, and destroy the Minerals. If it meete *chimiæ magna*
with them after consolidation, it will neuer be able to at- *lib.4.cap.8.*
tenuate them so, as to make them yeeld their qualities
to water. For wee neuer finde any Metals or Minerals
melted in the earth, which must be, if the heate of actuall fire were such as is imagined : neither doe wee euer

finde any floores of metall fublimed in the earth. This naturall heat is daily found by our Minerall men in the Mines,fo as oftentimes they are not able to touch them, as *Agricola* teftifieth ; although by opening their groues and admiffion of ayre,it fhould be wel qualified. Whereas on the other fide, it was neuer obferued, that any actuall kindled fire was euer feene by workmen in the earth, which were likely to be, if thefe fires were fo frequent.

Wherefore feeing we fee that Minerall waters do participate with all forts of Minerals,as well metals,as other, as hath beene fhewed in the particular examples of all of them: feeing alfo that few of them, vnleffe Minerall iuyces, are able to impart their quality to water,as they are confolidated, but only as they are *in folutis princi-pijs,* and whilft they are in generation, as is agreed vpon by all Authors : feeing alfo this naturall heat of fermentation muft neceffarily be prefent for the perfecting of their generations, and is fufficient, in regard of the degree of heat to make our Baths as hot as they are: feeing alfo that the other aduentitious fire,would rather deftroy thefe Minerals, then further them : feeing alfo we cannot imagine it either likely, or poffible, without manifold difficulties, and abfurdities : I doe conclude that both the actuall heat of Baths, and the Minerall qualities which they haue, are deriued vnto them by meanes of this fermenting heat.

Examples might be brought from all kinde of generations, and from fome artificiall works, of this fermenting heat proceeding from the feeds of naturall *i, de pri-* things. Thefe feeds containing the fpecies, and kinds *ueratione.* of naturall bodies, are not from the Elements, but are placed in the Elements, where they propagate their fpecies, and indiuiduals, according to their nature ;

and haue their due times and feafons of appearing vpon
the Stage of the World. Animals haue their fet times
when their fpermatick fpirits are in turgefcence, fome
once, fome twice a yeare, and fome oftner : efpecially
in the fpring : *vere magis, quia vere calor redit offi-
bus* ; as *Virgill* fpeakes of Mares : only man in regard
of his excellency aboue other creatures, is not fo con-
finde.

Vegetables haue likewife their feafons of fetting and
planting, as they may haue the earth and the feafon
moft conuenient : yet at any time, if their feeds get
moyfture and heat to dilate them, they will ferment
and attempt the production of moe indiuiduals : but
oftentimes the Artift doth abufe this intention of nature, and conuerts it to his ends : and oftentimes nature
being fet in action to proceede *à potentia in actum*, doth
want conuenient meanes to maintaine her worke: as
when we fee a Ryck of Hay or Corne which hath receiued moyfture, burnt to afhes. So in the making of
Malt, or Woad, or Bread, or Beere, or Wine, &c. wee
make vfe of this generatiue fpirit for our ends : that we
may ftirre vp, and quicken it. Otherwife our Bread
would not be fo fauory, our Beere would be but Wort,
our Wine would bee but Muft, or Plumpottage, and
want thofe fpirits which we defire ; and which lie dead
and benumbed in the feeds, vntill they come to fermentation. And in all thefe there is an actuall heat, although it appeare not in liquid things, fo well as in dry:
becaufe it is there quenched, by the abundance of moyfture: yet we may obferue actiue Spirits in it, by the
bubling and hiffing, and working of it. So in minerals,
which as they haue this generatiue Spirit, for the pro-
pagation of their Species, as hath beene fhewed before,
fo they haue this meanes of fermentation, to bring them

from a potentiall qualitie, to an actuall exiftence: And
as their matter is more plentifull, and in confiftence
more hard and compact; fo thefe Spirits muft bee more
vigorous and powerfull to fubdue it : and confequently
the heate of their fermentation muft bee in a higher degree, then it is in other generations. And this is in briefe
(though rudely deliuered) mine opinion concerning the
actuall heate of our Bathes, and of the minerall qualities which we finde in them: which I referre to the cen-
fures of thofe that be learned.

There are two other motions which refemble this
fermentation. The one is *Motus Dilatationis*, the other
Antipatheticus. *Motus Dilatationis* is euident in Lyme,
in Allum, in Coperos, and other concrete iuyces,
where by the effufion of water, the Salt in the Lyme, or
the concrete iuyces being fuddenly diffolued, there is
by this motion, an actuall heate procured for a time, a-
ble to kindle any combuftible matter put to it.

The like we obferue in thofe Stone Coales, called metall Coales, which are mixed with a Marchefit containing fome minerall iuyce, which receiuing moyfture,
doth dilate it felfe, and growes fo hot, as oftentimes
great heapes of thofe Coales are kindled thereby, and
burnt before their time; as hath beene feene at Puddle
Wharfe in London, and at Newcaftle. But this is much
different from our fermentation.

Another *Motus* refembling this fermentation, is that
which is attributed to Antipathie, when difagreeing
fubftances being put together, doe fight, and make a
manifeft actuall heate; as Antimony and Sublimat, oyle
of Vitrioll, and oyle of Tartar, Allum Liquor and V-
rine, Lees, Chalke, &c. But the reafon of this difagree-
ment is in their Salts, whereof one is aftringent, the o-
ther relaxing; the one of eafie diffolution in water, the
other

other of hard diſſolution, &c. and not by reaſon of any
antipathie: for it is not likely that nature would produce
two contrarie ſubſtances mixed like atomes in one ſub-
ieét, but that in their very generations, the one would
be an impediment to the other. Moreouer if wee examine aright what this Sympathie and Antipathie is, we
ſhall finde it to be nothing but a refuge of ignorance,
when not being able to conceiue the true reaſons of
ſuch aétions, and paſſions in naturall things, wee flye
ſometimes to indefinite generalities, and ſometimes to
this inexplicable Sympathie and Antipathie: attributing
voluntaries, and ſenſitiue aétions and paſſions to inſen-
ſible ſubſtances. This *motus* alſo is much different from
fermentation, as may eaſily appeare by the former de-
ſcription. And thus much for this point of fermentation, which I hope will giue better ſatisfaétion then any
of the former opinions.

Cap. 14.

By what meanes it may be diſcouered what minerals a-
ny water containeth.

THe nature of minerals and their generations being
handled, and from thence the reaſons drawne, both
of the aétuall heate of Bathes, and of their qualities :
Now it is fit we ſhould ſeeke out ſome meanes, how to
diſcouer what minerals are in any Bath, that thereby we
may the better know their qualities, and what vſe to
make of them for our benefit. Many haue attempted this
diſcouery, but by ſuch weake meanes, and vpon ſuch
poore grounds, as it is no meruaile if they haue failed
of their purpoſe : for they haue contented themſelues
with a bare diſtillation or euaporation of the water, and

L obſeruing

obſeruing the ſediment, haue thereby iudged of the minerals, vnleſſe perhaps they finde ſome manifeſt taſte,
or ſmell, or colour in the water, or ſome vnctuous matter ſwimming aboue it. Some deſire no other argument
of Sulphur and Bitumen, but the actuall heate: as though
no other minerals could yeeld an actuall heate, but thoſe
two. But this point requires better conſideration; and I
haue beene ſo large in deſcribing the natures and generations of minerals, becauſe without it, wee cannot diſcerne what minerals we haue in our waters, nor iudge
of the qualities and vſe of them.

Our Minerals therefore, are either confuſed or mixed with the water. If they bee confuſed they are eaſily
diſcerned : for they make the water thick and pudly,
and will either ſwim aboue, as Bitumen will doe, or
ſinck to the bottome, as earth, Sulphur, and ſome terreſtriall iuyces; for no confuſed water will remaine long
vnſeparated. If they are perfectly mixed with the water, then their mixture is either corporall, where the
very body of the Minerall is imbibed in the water, or
ſpirituall, where either ſome exhalation, or ſpirit, or
tincture is imparted to the water.

Corporally there are no mineralls mixed with water, but iuyces, either liquid, as *ſuccus lapideſcens metallificus*, &c. before they are perfectly congeled into their
naturall conſiſtence, or concrete, as Salt, Niter, Vitriol,
and Allum. And theſe concrete iuyces doe not only diſſolue themſelues in water, but oftentimes bring with
them ſome tincture or ſpirit from other Minerals. For as water is apt to receiue iuyces, and tinctures,
and ſpirits from animals, and vegetables ; ſo are concrete iuyces, being diſſolued, apt to extract tinctures
and Spirits from minerals, and to communicate them
with water. And there are no Mynes, but haue ſome of

thefe concrete iuyces in them, to diffolue the materials
of them, for their better vnion and mixture: and there
are few minerals or metals, but haue fome of them incorporated with them: as we fee in Iron, and Copper,
and Tinne, and Leade, &c. And this is the reafon that
water being long kept in Veffels, of any of thefe metals,
it will receiue a tafte and fmell from them, efpecially if
it be attenuated, either by heate, or by addition of fome
foure iuyce; and yet more, if the metals be fyled into
powder, as we fee in making Chalibeat wine, or Sugar
of Leade, or Puttie from Tinne, or Verdegreafe from
Copper. There may be alfo a mixture of Spirituall fubftance from minerals, whilft they are in generation, and
in Solutis principijs : the water paffing through them,
and the rather if it be actually hot, for then it is more
apt to imbybe it, and will containe more in it, being attenuated by heate, then being cold; as we fee in Vrines,
which though they bee full of humours, yet make no
great fhew of them fo long as they are warme, but being
cold, doe fettle then to the bottome.

Thefe fpirituall fubftances are hardly difcerned in
our Baths, but by the effects; for they leaue no refidence
after euaporation; and are commonly as volutill in
fublimation as the water it felfe : neither doe they en-
creafe the weight of the water, nor much alter the tafte
or fmell of them, vnleffe they be very plentifull. Wherefore we haue no certaine way to difcouer them, but by
the effects. We may coniecture fomwhat of them by the
Mynes which are found neare vnto the Baths, and by
the mud which is brought with the water. But that
may deceiue, as comming from the paffages through
which the water is conueyed, or, perhaps, from the
fweat and ftrigments of mens bodyes which bathe in
them. The corporall fubftances are found, either by

fublima-

Sublimation or by precipitation. By Sublimation, when being brought to the ſtate of congelation, and ſtickes of Wood put into it, within a few dayes, the concrete iuyces will ſhoote vpon the wood; in Needles, if it bee Niter; in Squares, if it be Salt; and in Clods and Lumps, if it be Allum or Coperoſe; and the other minerall ſub-ſtance which the waters haue receiued, will either incor-porate a tincture with them, or if it be more terreſtriall, will ſettle and ſeparate from it, and by drying it at a gen-tle fire, will ſhew from what houſe it comes, either by colour, taſte, ſmell, or vertue : There is an other way by precipitation, whereby thoſe minerall ſubſtances are ſtricken downe from their concrete iuyces which held them, by addition of ſome oppoſite ſubſtance. And this is of two ſorts : either Salts, as Tartar, Soape, Aſhes, Kelps, Vrine, &c. Or ſowre iuyces, as Vinegar, Ly-mons, Oyle of Vitrioll, Sulphur, &c. In which I haue obſerued that the Salts are proper to blew colours, and the other to red: for example, take a piece of Scarlet cloath, and wet it in Oyle of Tartar (the ſtrongeſt of that kinde) and it preſently becomes blew: dip it a-gaine in Oyle of Vitriol, and it becomes red againe.

Theſe are the chiefe grounds of diſcouering minerall waters, according to which any man may make tryall of what waters he pleaſeth. I haue beene deſirous here-tofore to haue attempted ſome diſcouerie of our Bathes, according to theſe principals : but being thought (by ſome) either not conuenient, or not vſefull, I was wil-ling to ſaue my labour, which perhaps might haue ſee-med not to be worth thankes: and in theſe reſpects am willing now alſo to make but a bare mention of them.

C A P.

CAP.

Of the vse of Minerall waters, inwardly, outward-
ly. In this Chapter is shewed the inward vse of them,
first in generall; then particularly of the hot waters of
Bathe.

THe nature and generations of Minerals being handled, and how our Minerall waters receiue their im-
preſſions, and actuall heat from thence ; and by what
meanes they are to be tried, what Minerals are in each
of them. Now we are to ſhew the vſes of them ; which
muſt bee drawne from the qualities of the Minerals
whereof they conſiſt : which are ſeldome one or two,
but commonly moe. Theſe qualities are either the firſt,
as hot,cold,moyſt,& dry; or the ſecond, as penetrating,
aſtringent, opening, reſoluing, attracting,clenſing,mol-
lifying, &c. For the firſt qualities, it is certaine and a-
greed vpon by all Authors; That all Minerall waters
doe dry exceedingly, as proceeding from earth : but
ſome of thoſe doe coole withall, and ſome doe heat.

Cooling waters are good for hot diſtemperatures of
the liuer, ſtomach, kidneyes, bladder, wombe, &c. Alſo for ſalt diſtillations, ſharp humors, light obſtructions
of the Meſaraicks, &c.

Heating waters are good for cold affects of the ſtomach, bowels, wombe, ſeminary veſſels, cold diſtillations, Palſyes, &c.

For the ſecond qualities, clenſing waters are good in
all vlcers, eſpecially of the guts.

Mollifying waters, for all hard and ſchirrous tumors.

Aſtringent waters, for all fluxes, &c. and ſo of the
reſt.

Now

Now thefe waters are vfed either inwardly or outwardly.

Inwardly, either by mouth, or by iniection.

By mouth, either in potion, or in broaths, iuleps, &c.

6 de tuenda fanit. cap.9. *Galen* neuer vfed them inwardly, becaufe hee iudged their qualities to be difcouered by experience, rather then by reafon. And feeing we finde many of them to be venomous, and deadly, as proceeding from Arfenick, Sandaracha, Cadmia, &c. we had need bee very wary in the inward vfe of them.

Neptunes Well in Tarracina was found to be fo deadly, as it was therefore ftopped vp. By Monpellier at Perant is a Well which kils all the fowles that drinke of it; the lake Auernus kils the fowles that fly ouer it; fo doth the vapour arifing from Charons den betweene Naples and Puteolum. So there are diuers waters in Sauoy and Rhetia, which breede fwellings in the throat. Others proceeding from Gipfum doe ftrangle, &c. But where we finde waters to proceede from wholfome Minerals, and fuch as are conuenient, and proper for our intents, there we may be bold to vfe them as well inwardly as outwardly: yet fo as we doe not imagine them to bee fuch abfolute remedies, as that they are of themfelues able to cure difeafes without either rules for the vfe of them, or without other helps adioyned to them. For as it is not enough for a man to get a good Damafco or Bilbo blade to defend himfelfe withall, vnleffe he learne the right vfe of it, from a Fencer; fo it is not enough to get a medicine and remedy for any difeafe, vnleffe it be rightly vfed, and this right vfe muft come from the Phyfitian, who knowes how to apply it, and how to prepare the body for it, what to adde and ioyne with it, how to gouerne and order the vfe of it, how to preuent fuch inconueniences as may happen by it, &c.

Wherefore, where we fpeake of any Minerall water, or of any other medicine that is proper for fuch & fuch a griefe, we muft be fo vnderftood, that the medicine is wife enogh to cure the difeafe of it felfe, no more then a fword is able of it felfe to defend a man, or to offend his enemy, but according to the right and skilfull vfe of it. And as it is not poffible for a Fencer to fet down abfolute rules in writing for his Art, whereby a man may be able in reading of them to defend himfelfe ; no more is the Phyfitian poffibly able to direct the particular vfes of his remedy, whereby a patient may cure himfelfe without demonftration and the paticular direction of the Phyfitian. It is true, that we haue generall rules to guide vs in the cure of difeafes, which are very true and certaine ; yet when we come to apply them to particular perfons, and feuerall conftitutions, thefe generall rules are not fufficient to make a cure, but is iuftly varied according to circumftances. Hereupon we daily finde, that thofe patients which thinke to cure themfelues, out of a little reading of fome rules or remedies, are oftentimes dangeroufly deceiued. And this is enough to intimate generally concerning the vfes of our Minerall waters.

Inwardly we finde great and profitable vfe of fuch waters as proceed from Niter, Allum, Vitriol, Sulphur, Bitumen, Iron, Copper, &c. Examples whereof I haue fet downe before in the feuerall Minerals, referring the particular vfes of each to fuch Authors as haue purpofely defcribed them.

My intent is chiefely to apply my felfe to thofe Baths of Bath in Summerfetfhire ; which confifting, as I iudge, principally of Bitumen, with Niter, and fome Sulphur, I hold to be of great vfe both inwardly and outwardly. And I am forry that I dare not commend
the

the inward vſe of them as they deſerue, in regard I can
hardly be perſwaded that we haue the water pure, as
the ſprings yeeld them, but doe feare, leſt where wee
take them, they may bee mixt with the water of the
Bath. If this doubt were cleared, I ſhould not doubt
to commend them inwardly, to heat, dry, mollifie,
diſcuſſe, glutinate, diſſolue, open obſtructions, cleanſe
the kidneyes, and bladder, eaſe cholicks, comfort the
matrix, mitigate fits of the mother, helpe barrenneſſe
proceeding from cold humors, &c. as *Tabernemontanus*
affirmes of other Bitumious Baths. Alſo in regard of
the Niter, they cut and diſſolue groſſe humors, and
cleanſe by vrine. In regard of the Sulphur, they dry
and reſolue, and mollifie, and attract, and are eſpecially
good for vterine effects proceeding from cold and win-
dy humors. Our Bath Guides do uſually commend the
drinking of this water with ſalt to purge the body, per-
ſwading the people, that the Bath water hath a purging
quality in it, when as the ſame proportion of ſpring water, with the like quantity of ſalt will doe the like. Our
Baths haue true virtues enough to commend them, ſo
as we need not ſeeke to get credit or grace vnto them
by falſe ſuggeſtions. The Bitumen and Niter which is
in them, although it ſerues well for an alteratiue remedy, yet it is not ſufficient for an euacuatiue : and therefore we muſt attribute this purgatiue quality, either to
the great quantity of water which they drink (and ſo it
works) *ratione ponderis*) or vnto the ſtimulation of ſalt
which is diſſolued in it, or vnto both together. I
ſhould like much better to diſſolue in it ſome appropri-
ate ſirrup or other, purgatiue, for this purpoſe, as Manna,
Tartar, Elaterium, ſirrups of Roſes, of Cicory, with
Rhewbarb, Auguſtunus : or to moue vrine, *Syr. de 5.*
rad, Bizantinus de Limonibus, Sambucinus de Althea,
                                                            &c.

&c. And this courſe is vſuall in Italy, according as the Phyſitian ſees moſt conuenient, but with this caution, that when they take it in potion, they muſt not vſe the Bath, becauſe of contrary motions.

Inwardly alſo Bath waters are vſed, for Brothes, Beere, Iuleps, &c. although ſome doe miſlike it, becauſe they will not mixe medicaments with aliments : wreſting a text in *Hippocr*. to that purpoſe. But if wee may mixe Diureticks, Deoppilatiues, Purgatiues, &c. with aliments, as vſually we doe. I ſee no reaſon but we may as well vſe minerall waters, where we deſire to make our aliments more alteratiue by a medicinall qualitie: alwaies prouided that there be no malignitie in them, nor any ill qualitie which may offend any principall part. And thus much for the vſe of them by mouth.

By iniection they are vſed alſo into the Wombe, to warme and dry, and cleanſe thoſe parts; into the paſſages of vrine, to drie and heale excoriations there : into the fundament for the like cauſes, as alſo for reſolutions of the Sphincter, and bearing downe of the fundament, &c. And thus they are vſed either alone, or mixed with other medicines, according as the Phyſitian thinks moſt fit, and we daily finde very good ſucceſſe thereby in vterin effects, depending vpon cold cauſes. Thus much for the inward vſe of our Bath waters.

M   CAP:

Cap. 16.

Of the outward vſe of the hot waters of Bathe; firſt, the generall vſe of them to the whole body, in bathing : ſecondly, the particular vſe of them, by pumping, bucketing, or applying the mud.

Ovtwardly our Bath waters are principally vſed, becauſe they are moſt properly for ſuch effects, as are in the habit of the body, and out of the veines: As Palſies, Contractions, Rheumes, cold tumours, affects of the skin, aches, &c. And in theſe caſes we vſe not onely the water, but alſo the mudde, and in ſome places the vapour.

The water is vſed both for his actuall and potentiall heate, as alſo for the ſecond qualities of mollifying, diſcuſſing, clenſing, reſoluing, &c. which the minerals giue vnto it. The vſe hereof is either generall to the whole body, as in bathing, or particular, to ſome one part, as in bucketting or pumping, which anciently was called *Stillicidium*. The Italians call it *Duccia*. The generall vſe in Bathing, is moſt ancient : for our Bathes were firſt diſcouered thereby to be wholeſome and ſoueraigne in many diſeaſes.

*Necham*s verſes concerning the vſe of theſe Bathes, are foure hundred yeares old:

Bathoniæ Thermas vix præfero Virgilianas
Confecto proſunt Balnea noſtra ſeni :
Proſunt attritis, colliſis inualidiſque
Et quorum morbis frigida cauſa ſubeſt.

Which I will Engliſh out of Maſter Doctor *Hackwels* learned worke, of the perpetuitie of the world.

Our Baynes at Bathe with *Virgils* to compare;
For their effects, I dare almoſt be bold,
For feeble folke, and crazie good they are,
For bruis'd, confum'd, farre ſpent, and very old,
For thoſe likewiſe whoſe ſickneſſe comes of cold.

We haue antient traditions *(fama eſt obſcurior annis)*
That King *Bladud* who is ſaid to haue liued in the time
of *Elias*, did firſt diſcouer theſe Bathes, and made tryall
of them vpon his owne ſonne, and thereupon built this
Citie, and diſtinguiſhed the Bathes, &c. But we haue no
certaine record hereof. It is enough that wee can ſhew
the vſe of them for 4000. yeares, and that at this day
they are as powerfull as euer they were: *Camden* giues
them a more ancient date from *Ptolomy* and *Antonin*,
and the Saxons: and ſaith they were called *Aqua Solis*,
and by the Saxons *Akmancheſter*, that is, the towne of
ſicke people, and dedicated to *Minerua*, as *Solinus* ſaith.
The opinion that the Bathes were made by Art, is too
ſimple for any wiſe man to beleeue, or for me to confute:
And *Necham* in his verſes which follow after thoſe I
haue mentioned, doth hold it a figment: you may ſee
them in *Camden*. We haue them for their vſe in bathing,
diſtinguiſhed into foure ſeuerall Bathes, whereof three
haue beene anciently: namely the Kings Bath, the hot
Bath, and the Croſſe Bath. The Queenes Bath was taken
from the Springs of the Kings Bath, that being farther
off, from the hot Springs, it might ſerue for ſuch as
could not endure the heate of the other. We haue likewiſe an appendix to the hot Bath, called the Leapers
Bath, for vncleane perſons. We finde little difference in
the nature of theſe Bathes, but in the degree of heate,
proceeding no doubt, from one and the ſame Myne.
Yet as the Myne may be hotter in one part then in an

other, or the paſſages more direct from it, ſo the heate
of them may vary. Some little difference alſo we finde
among them, that one is more cleanſing then another,
by reaſon (as I take it) of more Niter. For in the croſſe
Bath wee finde that our fingers ends will ſhrinke and
ſhriuell, as if we had waſhed in Soape water, more then
in the other Bathes. The Kings Bath, as it is the hotteſt
of all the Bathes, ſo it is the fitteſt for very cold diſeaſes,
and cold and plegmaticke conſtitutions: And we haue
daily experience of the good effects it worketh vpon
Palſies, Aches, Sciaticaes, cold tumours, &c. both by
euacuation, by Sweate, and by warming the parts affe-
cted, attenuating, diſcuſſing, and reſoluing the humors:
Alſo in Epilepſies and Vterin affects in the Scorbut, and
in that kinde of dropſie which wee call Anaſarca. The
hot Bath is little inferiour vnto it, as next in degree of
heate, and vſefull in the ſame caſes. The Queenes Bath,
and Croſſe Bath are more temperate in their heate, and
therefore fitteſt for tender bodies, which are apt to bee
inflamed by the other, and where there is more neede
of mollifying and gentle warming, then of violent heate
and much euacuation by ſweate. And in theſe Bathes
they may indure longer without diſſipation of Spirits,
then in the other: the Queenes Bath is the hotter of the
two, but temperate enough for moſt bodies. The Croſſe
Bath is the coldeſt of all, as hauing but few Springs to
feede it: yet we obſerue it to ſupple, and mollifie more
then the reſt, both becauſe they are able to ſtay longer
in it, and becauſe (as I ſaid before) it ſeemes to participate more with Niter, then the reſt, which doth cleanſe
better, and giues more penetration to the other Minerals. Wherefore in contractions, Epilepſies, Vterin affects, Conuulſions, Cramps, &c. This Bath is very
vſefull, as alſo in cutaneall diſeaſes, as Morphewes,
Itch.

Itch, &c. Thus much for the nature and difference of our Bathes, and the generall vſe of them in bathing.

They are vſed alſo to particular parts by pumping or bucketting, or applying the mud.

Pumping or bucketting are not vſed in that faſhion, as we vſe them, in any other Baths that I can learne, but only the Duccia or Stillicidium : But I hold our faſhion as good as that. The water comes more plentifully vpon the part, and may be directed as the patient hath occaſion. Our bucketting hath beene longeſt in vſe : but finding that it did not heat ſome ſufficiently, being taken from the ſurface of the Bath. We haue of late erected Pumpes, which draw the water from the ſprings or neare vnto them, ſo as wee haue it much hotter from thence, then wee can haue it by bucketting. A worthy Merchant and Citizen of London, M. *Humphrey Browne*, was perſwaded by me to beſtow two of theſe Pumps vpon the Kings and Queenes Bath, whereby he hath done much good to many, and deſerues a thankfull remembrance. The like alſo I procured to be done at the other Baths, although that of the Croſſe Bath is not ſo vſefull, by reaſon it wants heat, vnleſſe for yong children. Alſo we haue a Pumpe out of the hot Bath, which wee call the dry Pumpe, where one may ſit in a chayre in his clothes, and haue his head, or foot, or knee pumped without heating the reſt of the body in the Bath ; and deuiſed chiefely for ſuch as haue hot kidneys, or ſome other infirmities which the Bath might hurt. This we finde very vſefull in rheumes and cold Braines, and in aches or tumors in the feet. For theſe Pumps we are beholding vnto the late Lord Archbiſhop of Yorke, and to M. *Hugh May*, who vpon my perſwaſions were contented to bee at the charge of them. It were to be wiſhed that ſome well diſpoſed to the publique good, would erect the like at the Kings Bath, where, perhaps, it might be more vsefull for many, in regard of the greater heat which those springs haue.

The lute of Baths, is in much vse in some places, where it may be had pure, both to mollifie, and to resolue, and to strengthen weake parts. But we make little vse of it in our Baths, because we cannot haue it pure, but mixed with strigments. In diuers other places either the springs arise a good distance from the bathing places, or else there be other eruptions from whence it may bee taken. But our springs arising in the Baths themselues, it cannot well be saued pure. Besides, we haue not those meanes of the heat of the Sunne, to keepe it warme to the parts where it is applyed : so as growing cold, it rather does hurt then good. Wherefore it were better for vs, to vse artificiall lutes, as the Ancients did, of clay, Sulphur, Bitumen, Niter, Salt, &c. or vnguents of the same nature, as that which they call Ceroma. But the best way is to referre the election of these remedies, to the present Physitian, who will fit them according to the nature of the griefe.

CAP. 17.

In what particular infirmities of body, bathing in the hot waters of Bath is profitable.

TO come more particularly to the vse of bathing, we must vnderstand, that there are many Minerall waters fit for bathing, which are not fit to drinke : as those which participate with Lead, Quickfiluer, Gypsum, Cadmia, Arsenick, &c. Also those that containe liquid Bitumen, are thought to relaxe too much : but those

those that proceede from dry Bitumen, are permitted, and prescribed in potion, by *Paulus Ægineta*, and *Trallian* : Sulphur also is questioned, whether it bee fit to be taken inwardly by potion, because it relaxeth the stomach, and therefore *Aetius* forbids it : yet *Trallian* allowes it, and so doe others, if the Sulphur be not predominant. But for outward bathing there is no question to be made of these Minerals, nor of any other which are not in themselues venomous. And whereas *Oribasius*, *Ægineta*, *Actuarius*, &c. are suspicious of Sulphur and Bitumen for the head ; they must bee vnderstood of hot distempers there, and not of cold rheumatick braines ; where by daily experience wee finde the profitable vse of them, both by euacuation in bucketting, and by warming and comforting the cold part. And *Oribasius* doth ingenuously confesse, that the nature of these Baths was not then perfectly discouered : and therefore they were all held to bee, not only dry, but very hot : although we finde them not all so : for, Iron waters doe coole, and so doe those of Campher, and Alluminous, and Nitrous waters also. But for our Bitumious and Sulphurous waters, which *Galen* forbids in hot braines, there is no reason to suspect them in cold effects of the braine and nerues, in which cases we make especiall choyce all things, which either in taste or smell doe resemble Bitumen : as Rue, Castorum, *Valeriana, herba paralyseos, trifolium, asphalitis, &c* ; which both by his warming quality, and by his suppling and mollifying substance, is most proper and conuenient for those parts. The like I may say of Sulphur, in which nothing can bee excepted against, but his sharp spirit, which is made by burning : and wee haue none of that in our waters, nor, I hope, any fire to make it withall. The other parts of Sulphur are hot and

1 Tretrab. serm. 3. cap. 167. Trallian l. 10. c. 11

Orib. l. 10. c. 31 Ægin. l. 1. c. 52: Actuar. l. 3. c. 10

cap. 51

Hippoc. de aere, aquis, & locis.

de sanit. tuenda lib. 6. cap. 9.

and dry, and very vnctuous. As for Niter, it clenseth, purgeth both by stoole and vrine, and helpeth the incorporation of the other Minerals with the water, and qua lifies the heat of them, and giues them better penetration into our bodies. In regard of these Minerals, together wi h the actuall heat, we finde that the bathing in our Baths doth warme the whole habit of the body, attenuate humors, open the pores, procure sweat, moue vrine, cleanse the matrix, prouoke womens euacuations, dry vp vnnaturall humors, strengthen parts weakned, comfort the nerues, and all neruous parts, cleanse the skin, and suck out all salt humors from thence, open obstructions if they be not too much impacted, ease paines of the ioynts, and nerues, and muscles, mollifie and discusse hard tumors, &c. Whereby this bathing is profitable for all palsies, apoplexies, caros, epylepsies, stupiditie, defluctions, gouts, sciaticaes, contractions, cramps, aches, tumors, itches, scabs, leprosies, collicks, windines, whites in women, stopping of their courses, barrennesse, abortions, scorbuts, anasurcas, and generally all cold and phlegmatick diseases, which are needlesse to reckon vp. In all which cures our Bathes haue a great hand, being skillfully directed by the Physitian, with preparation of the body before, and addition of such other helps as are needfull. And whereas without the helpe of such Baths these diseases could not be cured without tormenting the body, either by fire, or launcing, or causticks, or long dyets, or bitter and vngratefull medicines, &c. In this course of bathing all is pleasant and comfortable, and more effectuall then the other courses, and therefore it is commonly the last refuge in these cases, when all other meanes faile. I will not vndertake to reckon vp all the benefits which our Baths doe promise; but if wee had a register kept of the

　　　　　　　　　　　　　　　　　　　manifold

manifold cares which haue beene done by the vſe of our
Bathes principally, it would appeare of what great vſe
they are. But as there is a defeſt in not keeping a Cata-
logue of rare Cures, ſo many perſons of the better ſort
would be offended if a Phyſitian ſhould make any mention of their cures or griefes: wherefore I muſt ſpeake
but generally.

Cap. 18.

*The manner of bathing, chiefly referred to the inſpe-
ction and ordering of a Phyſician. Yet ſome particulars
touched, concerning the gouernement of the Patient in
and after bathing: the time of day, of ſtaying in the Bathe,
of continuing the vſe of it. The time of the yeare. Of couering the Baths.*

NOw for the manner of Bathing, I will not ſet downe
what the Phyſitian is to doe, but leaue that to his
iudgement and diſcretion: but what is fit for the Patient to know: for there are many cautions and obſerua-
tions in the vſe of bathing, drawne from the particular
conſtitutions of bodies; from the complication of diſeaſes, and from many other circumſtances which cannot be comprehended in generall rules, nor applied to
all bodies alike: But many times vpon the ſucceſſe, and
the appearing of accidents, the Phyſitian muſt *ex re na-
ta capere conſilium*, and perhaps alter his intended
courſe, and perhaps change the Bath either to a hotter
or cooler, &c. In which reſpeſt, thoſe Patients are ill
aduiſed which will aduenture without their Phyſitian
vpon any particular Bath, or to direſt themſelues in the
vſe of it. And this is a great cauſe that many goe away
from hence without benefit, and then they are apt to

complaine of our Bathes, and blafpheme this great blef-
fing of God beftowed vpon vs.

It is fit for the Patient when he goeth into the Bath,
to defend thofe parts which are apt to be offended by
the Bath: as to haue his Head well couered from the
ayre and winde, and from the vapours arifing from the
Bath: alfo his kidneyes (if they be fubieƈt to the Stone)
anoynted with fome cooling vnguents; as *Rofatum co-*
mitiffæ infrigidans Galeni fantolinum, &c. Alfo to begin
gently with the Bath, till his body be inured to it, and
to be quiet from fwimming, or much motion, which
may offend the Head by fending vp vapours thither: at
his comming forth, to haue his body well dryed, and
to reft in his Bed an houre, and fweate, &c.

A morning houre is fitteft for Bathing, after the funne
hath bin vp an houre or two; and if it be thought fit to
vfe it againe in the afternoone, it is beft foure or fiue
houres after a light dinner. For the time of ftaying in
the Bath, it muft bee according to the qualitie of the
Bath, and the tolleration of the Patient. In a hot Bath, an
houre or leffe may be fufficient: in a temperate Bath, two
houres. For the time of continuing the Bath, there can
be no certaine time fet downe, but it muft be according
as the Patient findes amendment, fometimes twenty
dayes, fometimes thirty, and in difficult cafes much longer. And therefore they reckon without their Hoft,
which affigne themfelues, a certaine time, as perhaps
their occafions of bufineffe will beft afford. For the time
of the yeare, our Italian and Spanifh Authors preferre
the Spring and Fall; and fo they may well doe in their
hot Countries; but with vs confidering our clymat is
colder, and our Bathes are for cold difeafes; I hold the
warmeft moneths in the yeare to be beft; as May, Iune,
Iuly, and Auguft; and I haue perfwaded many hereun-

to who haue found the benefit of it; for both in our Springs, and after September, our weather is commonly variable, and apt to offend weake persons; who finding it temperate at noone, doe not suspect the coolenesse of the mornings and euenings. Likewise in the Bath it selfe, although the Springs arise as hot as at other times, yet the winde and ayre beating vpon them, doth doe them much harme, and also make the surface of the water much cooler then the bottome: and therefore *Claudinus* wisheth all Bathes to be couered, and *Fallopius* findes great fault with the Lords of Venice, that they doe not couer their Bath at Apono. Wee see also that most of the Bathes in Europe, are couered, whereby they retaine the same temperature at all times. And it were to be wished that our Queenes Bath, and Crosse Bath, being small Bathes, were couered, and their Slips made close and warme. By this meanes our Bathes would be vsefull all the yeare, when neither winde and cold ayre in winter, nor the Sunne in summer, should hinder our bathing. Moreouer for want of this benefit, many who haue indifferently wel recouered in the Fall, doe fall backe againe in the winter before the Cure bee perfectly finished : and as this would be a great benefit to many weake persons, so it would be no harme to this Citie, if it may be a meanes of procuring more respect hither in the Winter time, or more early in the Spring, or more late at the Fall. The Right Honourable, the Earle of *Marleborow*, hath of his owne accord and noble disposition to doe any Bathes good, vndertaken the couering of the Crosse Bath vpon his sole charge. If some other out of the like affection would doe the like for the Queenes Bath, they should doe much good to many, and gaine a thankefull remembrance to their names for euer.

I defire not nouelties, or to bring in innouations, but I propound thefe things vpon good grounds and examples of the beft Bathes in Europe, and fo I defire to haue them confidered of; referring both this point, and whatfoeuer elfe I haue faid in this difcourfe, to the cenfure of thofe who are able to iudge.

I doe purpofely omit many things about the vertues and vfes of our Bathes, which belong properly to the Phyfitian, and cannot well be intimated to the Patient *De compof. med.* without dangerous miftaking. For as *Galen* faith, our *f. locos lib. 8. c. 7.* Art of Phyficke goes vpon two legges, Reafon and Experience, and if either of thefe be defectiue, our Phyficke muft needs be lame. Reafon without Experience, makes a meere contemplatiue and theoricall Phyfitian: Experience without Reafon, makes a meere Empericke, no better then a Nurfe or an attendant vpon ficke perfons, who is not able out of all the experience he hath, to gather rules for the cure of others. Wherefore they muft be both ioyned together: and therefore I referre Phyfitians workes, vnto Phyfitians themfelues.

F I N I S.

Errata.

Page 2. line 19. for 4000. reade 40000. page 83. line 13: for 4000. reade 400.